America's Cup Fever

America's Cup Fever

An Inside View of Fifty Years of
America's Cup Competition

by Bob Bavier

Yachting Books/Ziff-Davis Publishing Company/New York

Ziff-Davis Publishing Company
One Park Avenue
New York, N.Y. 10016

Contents

Foreword

Because my own involvement with America's Cup competition happens to coincide precisely with the period on which this account is focused, and because during that period I was fortunate to become acquainted with many of the leading characters of that period, I can say with conviction that the author is "spot on" throughout the text.

In addition, circumstances placed me very close, both physically and mentally, during the key part of an unforgettable campaign—*Constellation* 1964. I have some insight in how Bob Bavier, the sailor and the author, is so highly successful.

I also had the good fortune of knowing Bob's parents—during what would be called a formative period—and both Olin and I had respect and admiration for them and learned many important basics of sailing from Bob, Sr., who clearly earned the name some of us had for him—The Brain.

One particular detail was Bob Sr.'s clear explanation of the relative merits of yawl versus ketch, which has helped keep me on course in an area where there is more than a little misunderstanding. Neither Bob Sr., nor his son have ever forgotten the importance of sailing efficiently and, still more important, enjoying it.

During my involvement with *Constellation* in '64, I continued to learn from the author. It has been my good fortune to sail with many wonderful helmsmen, but none who could get a boat from one tack to the other with less loss of speed or with an easier job for the crew.

The way Bob could delegate responsibility reminded me of Tom Watson, whose success with I.B.M. has certainly been helped by the most successful application of this skill. Bob never second guesses his tactical advisors, nor his navigator, and the way he would walk up the dock for dinner in the evening with his family, even when there were relatively intricate mechanical details to sort out before an early harbor start the next morning, emphasizes this ability. This practice had astonishingly beneficial results.

First and foremost, Bob always arrived on board for the next race with the benefit of having had an enjoyable and relaxed evening, plus a good night's sleep, so that *Constellation* always had the benefit of his best potential.

Meanwhile, the nut and bolt boys realized that the ball was in their court, so they gave it all they had and again and again, jobs were done better and quicker than would have been possible if the "old man" was asking questions and complicating the situation with various alternative possibilities.

This delegation of responsibility did much to build mutual trust and confidence among the various components that very rapidly became an efficient crew. The relation between skipper, navigator, tactician, midship crew and those on the foredeck was never strained and this did much to provide a successful end result.

With such appropriate basic credentials, Bob has been able to clearly explain so much relating to the key personalities including enlightening information on designers and also helmsmen, and wonderfully clear explanations of key races and tactics involved.

When I read Bob's comments on the "black box", it seemed almost like E.S.P.—almost as though I should have credit for writing from that particular viewpoint; likewise "Why Twelve Meters?"

Bob's great understanding of right-of-way rules permits him to provide vividly clear explanations of pivotal protests—particularly the '34 and '70 matches, and the latter are documented by an excellent sequential series of pictures.

I would like to add small personal comments on four of the designers Bob has chronicled so appropriately.

I was introduced to Capt. Nat Herreshoff by Mike Vanderbilt in the middle of the 1937 campaign. My job was to show and explain some movies of *Ranger* and some of her competitors in Capt. Nat's home, where he was bedridden at the time. However, Capt. Nat proved to be one person who had such complete basic knowledge that he clearly saw more in the pictures than either Mike Vanderbilt or I had seen, and after I had made a few introductory explanations, both Mike Vanderbilt and I were able to sit back and listen to the myriad of details that that wonderful man spotted with such immediate precision and clarity. At that occasion, I realized that one could not possibly exaggerate his capabilities and his contributions to all types of nautical development, all of which was well corroborated by contacts with his son Sydney, and later with his grandson, Halsey.

Mike Vanderbilt was also responsible for my contact with Starling Burgess during the design, construction and sailing of *Ranger.* There was no possible doubting Starling Burgess' credentials, but what really impressed me was his willingness to share his great knowledge with his co-designer, my brother Olin. The alacrity with which Mr. Burgess could reach the bottom line was so clearly demonstrated when he solved a complex raking problem aloft on *Enterprise,* when she was in danger of losing her mast, by quickly clipping port and starboard spinnaker halyards over both middle and top shrouds to effectively tie these together and control the lower spreaders, which were overswinging by failure of the gear which secured them.

Olin has been given deserved credit for his amply demonstrated skill in the field of yacht design and I would like to add that while I have been lucky enough to sail with many of the very best, there is no better shipmate whether it's around the buoys or a hard offshore sail, nor is there a better tactitian, nor one more knowledgeable in sail analysis, weather judgment, navigation, as well as a fine helmsman. Although *Mustang* was my own boat, she always did her best when Olin was aboard and at those times that he was skipper, and I moved down to mate—an arrangement which provided the best possible results.

Finally, while David Boyd did not achieve the desired results with *Sceptre* and *Sovereign,* we must not forget the great Six Meter *Circe* which he designed. She was the only Six to defeat *Goose* in the 1938 season. By coincidence, this match, which was for the Seawanhaka Cup, was the only 1938 series which Bob was unable to race aboard *Goose.*

Bob Bavier has given us a wonderfully perceptive, personal look at America's Cup competition. I hope others enjoy it as much as I did.

ROD STEPHENS

Preface

Much has been written about the America's Cup, some of it fascinating reading, some factual, some phony. Its history is so well chronicled that a rehash would be pointless. This book will focus instead on what I like to think of as the inside story of the last fifty years.

To present an inside story one has to have *been* inside, and in this respect I consider myself fortunate. My association with the America's Cup started in 1930 when my father was a member of the afterguard of the J-boat *Weetamoe,* one of the four candidates for defense. At the age of twelve I was aboard *Weetamoe* in an actual race, the youngest (to my knowledge) ever to race on a cup boat. Throughout the J-boat era in the 1930s I was a close spectator and got to meet and even know the participants. Since the renewal in 1958 of America's Cup racing in Twelve Meters, I have known the men who sailed in every successive match up to the present day. I know what it means both to win and lose, having been helmsman and "quarterback" of the defender *Constellation* in 1964 and skipper of the winning *Courageous* in 1974 up to the final race of the final trials when I was bounced in favor of Ted Hood. And to round off the picture, I was on the selection committee to pick the American defender in 1977 and will be again in 1980. Even when not directly involved I was on the scene, knew the players, saw and felt firsthand both the exhilaration of victory and the anguish of defeat in this grueling contest.

I will not go into the years prior to 1930 in any depth because to do so would depend on the written word or secondhand information, hardly the inside story I would like to tell. But for those readers who may be unfamiliar with the America's Cup races a capsule account of its history and significance might be of interest.

It all began in 1851 when the schooner yacht *America* sailed abroad to race against the best British yachts. It was like the Superbowl game between the New York Jets and the Baltimore Colts in 1969 when Namath and Company were given no chance but still won.

The United States was making seagoing history with its clipper ships in the mid-nineteenth century, but in yachting we were still a fledgling nation, while Britannia was conceived as ruling the waves. At that time we had but one yacht club, the New York Yacht Club, founded in 1844. We had no tradition and precious little experience in yacht racing, but John Stevens, commodore of the New York Yacht Club, was far from daunted. Yachts of that era were designed along the cod's head and mackerel tail configuration with full bows and long fine runs. *America,* on the other hand, was designed by George Steeres more along clipper ship lines with a fine entrance and powerful quarters. She was a refinement of the New York pilot boats which had to be both fast and seaworthy if they were to be the first to get a pilot aboard a ship entering New York harbor.

After a fast transatlantic passage, *America* put in at Le Havre, France, to be put into racing trim. When sailing from France to Cowes, England, she met one of England's fastest yachts and in an informal brush tipped her hand by sailing away from the British boat. This made it difficult for her to arrange matches which in those days were for substantial cash prizes or wagers. Finally she was allowed to enter a race around the Isle of Wight for what was then known as the 100 Guinea Cup. Arrayed against her was the cream of the English yachting fleet, yet *America* trounced them so thoroughly that Queen Victoria, when asking who was second, was told, "Alas, Your Majesty, there is no second."

Not only was *America*'s hull form revolutionary, but so also were her sails —far flatter and better able to hold their shape than the baggy sails carried by the British yachts. In all respects she was a breakthrough, and the magnitude of her triumph was such as to shatter the myth of England's yachting supremacy.

In 1857 the owners of *America* deeded their trophy, known ever since as the America's Cup, to the New York Yacht Club as an international challenge trophy. The first challenge came in 1870 when the schooner *Cambria* sailed to America in hopes of regaining the trophy. Like *America* she was forced to sail against a fleet of defenders, but unlike her she didn't come close to winning. She finished in the middle of the fleet, beaten even by the nineteen-year-old *America.* The winner was *Magic.*

The next year the schooner *Livonia* challenged, and in the interest of fairness she was compelled to sail against but one defender at a time. But the Americans didn't go overboard in being fair! Whereas *Livonia* now had to race only one boat at a time, two defenders *(Columbia* and *Sappho)* were selected, one to race if light air was expected, the other in a breeze. Again the Americans were easy winners, but rather than discouraging challenges, the beginning of a winning tradition was making the prize even more coveted.

Commencing with the 1876 match and forever after the races have been a true match race affair, with but one defender to meet the challenger.

The first three matches were between large schooners, but since 1881 only sloops and cutters have competed, the largest and still fastest on a reach being the 143-foot sloop *Reliance. Reliance* carried a huge sail plan of 15,000 square feet, double that of a J-boat and more than seven times the area carried by a Twelve Meter. It took a crew of forty-three to handle her. While a J-boat would have beaten her around the course because of its greater efficiency upwind, *Reliance* had the highest maximum speed of any cup boat. Her sail plan is shown on page 84.

While some matches were close, and while we even lost an occasional race in the competition which evolved into a best two out of three, then three out of five and finally a four out of seven series, the American boat was always the eventual winner.

In the 110 years since the first match and the 129 years since *America* sailed to glory, challenges have come from England, Canada, Scotland, Australia, France, and Sweden. There are no fewer than four different challengers for the twenty-fourth match in 1980. The longer the Americans continue to win, the greater incentive to be the first to beat us. I well remember watching the 1970 match between *Gretel II* and *Intrepid* with Tony Boyden who had backed *Sovereign*'s 1964 challenge against *Constellation*. I was a bit surprised to find him rooting for *Intrepid*. "But of course," said Tony, "I want to be the first to beat you bloody Americans."

Once bitten by America's Cup fever it is almost impossible to recover. Tony is behind the English challenge in 1980. The most persistent challenger was Thomas Lipton whose *Shamrock* challenged in 1899 and whose *Shamrock V* challenged in 1930, with three other *Shamrocks* making futile efforts in 1901, 1903, and 1920. Baron Bich of France first got bitten in 1970, but 1980 will mark his fourth effort to win the cup. The fact that his yachts have yet to win a single race in America's Cup trials has only made him redouble his efforts and spend even more millions of dollars in the quest of yachting's Holy Grail. If you think of Twelve Meters as large and glamorous boats, the drawings put them in proper perspective and reveal how gargantuan some of the earlier boats were.

Twelve Meters are large by today's standards, and they are also highly refined racing machines. The fact that they are impractical for anything but closed course racing and that each one costs at least one-and-a-half million dollars to design, build, and race for a single summer may be considered negatives by some. But these very impracticalities, combined with the fact that they are such superb performers, especially upwind, heightens the romance of the event. It is the one sailing contest which captures the imagination and the attention of the nonyachting public, the one event which any keen sailor would like to race in and win more than any other.

The America's Cup—a symbol of excellence, of man's striving to improve himself and his boat, and, especially in the case of challengers, a goal so unattainable as to kindle fierce desires, sacrifices, and effort in hopes of achieving it. It's the one unscaled Mount Everest in the world of sport, and people don't laugh when it is called the greatest sporting event in the world.

It's worth looking into, so with no further ado, let's get started.

Chapter 1
A 1930 Race on Weetamoe

It was a beautiful day in the early summer of 1930 as I steamed down Long Island Sound on a Fall River liner bound for Buzzards Bay. But I wasn't very happy. The year before, when I was eleven, my dad had bought me a Bullseye Class sloop, otherwise known as a Herreshoff 12½ (for her water-line length). I had great fun racing her and even took a few overnight cruises with a friend my own age. It had been the best summer of my life. I thought I was a pretty hot sailor and was looking forward to more of the same.

It came as a shock to me, therefore, when I was told in the spring of 1930 that I was going to camp on Buzzards Bay. The fact that Camp Mashnee was supposed to have a good sailing program (I later found out it didn't—the boats, like those at all camps of my acquaintance, where pretty poor and no match for my Bullseye) didn't sell me. But my parents told me it was an opportunity most boys would leap at, I would have lots of fun, meet new friends, and, besides, it would be good for me to have a summer away from home.

1

When none of these arguments came close to convincing me, I was finally told the real reason. My dad had been asked to be part of the afterguard on the J-boat *Weetamoe,* one of four American boats vying for the right to defend the America's Cup, and would be away all summer. I couldn't tag along without being in the way and couldn't stay home alone.

Being brought up in a family where sailing monopolized most of our thoughts and conversation, even at age twelve I knew something about the importance of the America's Cup. I was excited about Dad being part of it, but at that age my own boat seemed more important. That's why I felt a bit put upon and more than a little homesick as we steamed east.

Camp Mashnee turned out fine, and, despite its typical camp fleet of boats, I had fun not only sailing but in all other camp activities. Even so, the weekly highlight was a letter from Dad.

He was never a prolific letter writer, but that summer I received a brief note from him at least once a week telling me about the races between *Weetamoe* and the other three contenders: *Enterprise, Yankee,* and *Whirlwind.* The news was usually good since *Weetamoe* had the best record in the early races. I remember Dad cautioning me not to be too optimistic—saying that the final races in the latter part of August were all that really counted and that by then the others, especially *Enterprise,* might find themselves. I dismissed this as just so much adult conservatism and found it hard to conceive any boat my dad had a key role in failing at the end after such a strong start. I felt pretty good about the whole thing except that I would have liked to see them race.

A Race on Weetamoe

At the beginning of August a letter arrived with the exciting news that the J-boats would be sailing on the New York Yacht Club cruise and on 5 August would be racing on Buzzards Bay off Mattapoisett, just a few miles from my camp. I thought the next lines would read that I could get a chance to watch them race. Instead Dad wrote that he had squared it with both *Weetamoe*'s skipper George Nichols and with the director of the camp for me actually to race on board *Weetamoe.* I let out a clarion yell which might still be reverberating on the eastern reaches of Buzzards Bay.

The morning of the race was sparkling with a light-to-moderate NNW wind ruffling the waters of Buzzards Bay. I felt like a big shot as *Weetamoe*'s tender with my dad standing in the bow eased alongside our dock at camp to take me on board. But as we neared *Weetamoe* I began to feel even smaller than my four feet four and seventy-three pounds. Her freeboard was five and a half feet and I had to climb rather than step aboard. Dad introduced me first to George Nichols and the rest of the afterguard, all resplendent in white flannels, white shoes, and yachting jackets. "Mr." Nichols, as I thought of him then (and ever after, even when I was to crew with him eight years later on the Six Meter *Goose* to win the Scandinavian Gold Cup), couldn't have been nicer. He shook my hand, smiled with all his face and eyes, and told me how glad he was that I had come for the race and that if I was anything like my dad I would bring them luck. Though awed, I liked him immediately, and in subsequent years learned that my instinctive reaction was justified. There were better sailors than George Nichols but no better nor kinder men.

Dad introduced me to many of the crew, all decked out in spotless white sailor suits. I remember most the callouses on their hands as I shook them —hard as concrete and equally rough. They were polite in a hearty way but, I sensed, a bit surprised that such a young squirt would be allowed aboard for a real race. The part of their "uniform" that most intrigued me was a hank of cotton string looped through a leather thong at their waists and then braided. Dad told me that these were for stopping the light sails.

Dad told me about one particular brute of a man I had just met. He had been swept overboard the day before on the hard reach from Newport to Mattapoisett. *Weetamoe* was battling for the lead at the time, and as the crewman came to the surface, he hollered—"Keep going, I can swim to shore;" this despite the fact that the nearest shore was three miles away and no boats were near. No one doubted his sincerity, but of course they went back for him and had him back aboard within minutes, none the worse for wear. When he complained, it was explained to him that a boat was disqualified if it finished without its full crew, which made him feel even worse for costing *Weetamoe* a possible victory. This man, whose name I unfortunately can't remember, epitomized the spirit of the entire crew—a tough, hearty group with as fierce a will to win as any crew I've ever seen. Perhaps they were influenced by the fact that every member of the professional crew received a cash bonus for each victory, and while I'm sure that motivated them, I felt then and still feel that pride was the main stimulant.

Perhaps Dad told me this story to warn me against the danger (and disgrace) of falling overboard but he gave me the dignity of not saying "Be careful." He showed me a place slightly behind the helmsman and the rest of the afterguard, as the amateur yachtsmen were called, which was to be my station for the race. I appreciated the fact that he didn't tell me to keep quiet, to ask no questions, and to be sure to keep out of the way once the race started. I knew enough about racing so that he didn't have to, but it made me feel more grown-up not to be so warned by him, "Mr." Nichols, or the others.

Dad also showed me below deck. I remember it as a cross between a machine shop and a storage warehouse, with huge cranks to activate the winches on deck, drums for lines, bins for an endless variety of enormous sails. More than anything else it seemed huge, extending seemingly forever and with headroom above a man's reach.

Weetamoe's larger tender came alongside soon after we were back on deck with the light weather main the afterguard had decided to use that day. It was flaked like a long sausage and more than twenty crew carried it aboard over their shoulders. I later learned it weighed over a ton. It took twenty minutes to bend on the main while we towed slowly out to the starting line. Several more minutes were required to hoist it, and I almost got dizzy craning my neck aloft as it went to the masthead more than 152 feet above deck.

We cast off and reached about under main alone, taking a compass bearing of the line and checking course signals. I could hear the navigator reporting that there was to be a 21-mile triangular course, a 10-mile beam

Weetamoe *making knots in 1930. That's my Dad standing by the main sheets. The crew member sitting furthest off is in the spot I occupied in the race off Mattapoisett.*

4

reach to FL White Bell "5" abeam of Robinsons Hole in the middle of Buzzards Bay, a slightly broader reach to a buoy near Falmouth, northeast of Woods Hole, and then a beat to the finish.

The leeward end of the line was favored, and I could hear the afterguard discussing which end to cross at. I remember to this day my dad recommending the leeward end and others suggesting the weather end on the assumption that *Weetamoe* was fast on a light reach and that all she needed was clear air. Dad countered by saying he expected the morning breeze to slacken before it freshened late in the day and that if the wind did die it would be important to be to leeward and thus able to increase speed by heading higher late in the leg. Mr. Nichols listened to all hands, looked at the wind on the water, and then announced they would start at the windward end. My dad made no remonstrance, but I could swear he looked my way and gave me an imperceptible shrug and a wry grin. I, of course, said nothing but thought plenty, especially since Dad had castigated me on several occasions the previous summer for getting too high on a reach in light air and dying when I tried to get down to the mark.

Shortly after the warning gun we broke out our genoa and started reaching away from the line. At first *Weetamoe* seemed sluggish, but speed increased steadily, first five, then six, seven, eight, and then nearly nine knots despite a wind which couldn't have been over seven or eight. With five minutes to go we jibed back for the line on a tight reach. It looked like we might be okay, except that *Yankee* was just ahead of us and blanketing our wind. At the gun *Yankee* had a fine start at the weather end with *Weetamoe* a length behind. At the leeward end were *Whirlwind* and *Enterprise* in that order.

I remember our being luffed as we tried to pass *Yankee* to windward and the afterguard advising not to try again because we were getting too high. Down to leeward *Whirlwind* held her lead and rounded the first mark twelve seconds ahead of *Enterprise* with *Yankee* third one minute forty seconds later and Weetamoe ten seconds further back.

On the next reach *Whirlwind* set a ballooner with a small balloon staysail set inside it and had her finest leg of the entire summer. She drew away from *Enterprise* in startling fashion, until the latter set a staysail inside her genoa and thereafter did better. Unfortunately the wind up ahead was stronger and while we did pass *Yankee* after changing jibs (a long protracted operation), *Whirlwind*'s lead at the second mark was two minutes over *Enterprise,* nine over *Weetamoe,* and nine and a half over *Yankee.*

Whirlwind was sailing into a dying northerly with *Enterprise* gaining rapidly and *Weetamoe* and *Yankee* closing on both of them. Halfway up we had cut the deficit in half when I heard my Dad, without pointing but looking toward the west, saying, "There it is." No one else could see it but he had detected the first ruffling of a westerly. We tacked at once to starboard and as we did I too could see the new breeze.

We sailed for several lengths before the boats ahead tacked to cover but with *Yankee* close aboard. We switched to working sails just before the new breeze hit, tacked to port in the header, and started boiling for the line four miles away. Down to leeward I could see *Whirlwind* virtually flat and *Enterprise* little better off. *Weetamoe* heeled till her rail was just above the water. I had never seen water move past so fast, but what I remember most is the sound. There was a steady hiss as we sped along. *Weetamoe* seemed to be on a railroad track and a smooth one at that with no pitching whatsoever.

When our speed through the still smooth water had reached nearly eleven knots an oceangoing tug crossed our bow close aboard at full speed creating a huge quarter wave. As we approached the wave I looked for something to hang on to. I needn't have bothered. *Weetamoe*'s 143 tons sliced into the wave as though it wasn't there. There was no lurching, no loss in speed, just the barest nod of a lift to her long, lean bow as we smashed through the sea, throwing spray thirty feet to leeward. By the time the spray had settled we had left the wave astern. The feeling of power and of irresistible force is one I've never before or since even remotely experienced on any boat.

The excitement I felt by the speed of the graceful brute I was riding was heightened by the thrill of what had developed into a real race. *Yankee* was boiling along close astern but not really gaining. Down to leeward *Whirlwind* was still flat, now barely ahead of us and already behind *Enterprise*. For a while it appeared that we might sweep past *Enterprise* before she got into our breeze. We could see the wind approaching her but if it delayed just a few minutes more we might just sail around her. Then I saw her sails harden, saw her heel even before the wind on the water reached her, and knew we were too late. Sherman Hoyt, the wily member of Mike Vanderbilt's afterguard, was too smart to get too far out on a limb. While concentrating on passing *Whirlwind*, he had focused also on the boats behind and any new wind they might bring. As a result he had suggested to Mike that *Enterprise* match our tack even though it meant leaving *Whirlwind*, thus escaping the hole she sank into.

At the finish *Enterprise* beat us by more than two minutes. *Yankee* was eighteen seconds behind us and poor *Whirlwind* more than two and a half minutes further back.

I was too excited at sailing on such a magnificent machine and about our good last leg to feel any disappointment about not winning. Despite the long periods of light air we had averaged 8.57 knots for the course, which not only was the fastest I had traveled around a closed course but also ever since that momentous day fifty years ago.

After the finish the jib was dropped and George Nichols asked if I would like to steer for a moment. It must have been an incongruous sight to see me hanging onto that huge wheel and peering *between,* not over, the spokes. It was so finely geared, however, that I could turn it without too much effort, and when I turned, *Weetamoe*'s huge bulk responded. It would be thirty-four years before I would again touch the helm of a Cup contender in quite a different role.

Chapter II
America's Cup Skippers

One begins to appreciate the special significance of the America's Cup by scrutinizing the men who have raced for it. Not just by getting to know them but by exploring what it meant to them, the sacrifices they made, and the energies they squandered in the great pursuit. By probing the exhilaration they felt in victory and the depth of their despair in failure, we might begin to understand what makes the America's Cup so very special.

Many people feel it is easier to win the America's Cup than, say, a Star or Soling Class World Championship or an Olympic gold medal. There is some truth to this *once the competition begins,* simply because in a world championship or the Olympics there are scores of boats to beat, whereas in the America's Cup only two or three in the trials and only one opponent in the match itself. Hence through pure weight of numbers, there is a strong case for the claim that an Olympic medal is harder to win. Despite this the America's Cup remains the least attainable prize and the hardest to win for

Rod Stephens is never happier than when something needs fixing aloft.

two reasons. First, you cannot win it (or lose it) until or unless you are selected to be skipper or crew. And with almost every top sailor willing to give his eye teeth for the chance, the competition is fierce. Second, once selected, you are up against top sailors who got there because they were superbly qualified and had demonstrated their excellence in other major yachting events.

It is discouraging in a way but also stimulating and challenging to compete for the America's Cup and to know that the skippers and crews against you are going to sail superlatively well. One of the most fruitful ways to win in big fleets is to avoid mistakes, while waiting for your opponents to make errors in tactics, in helmsmanship, or in sail selection. Unless you have a much faster boat, that is a discouraging way to attempt to win in America's Cup competition. The other skippers and crew make so few mistakes and the ones they do make are so minor that you have got to be aggressive to win.

There have been a few examples in the past when men of wealth who were good but not brilliant sailors raced for the America's Cup because they were major contributors and to a certain degree bought themselves in. Not so any more. Only top sailors compete and very few top sailors who are asked decline the honor. One such is Buddy Melges, without question one of the world's finest sailors. But thus far, he has felt he could not take time away from business for the months on end required to become a defender. Watch for him to succumb in some future year.

Others who have been asked either beat their bosses over the head until they give in, take a leave of absence without pay, or, in more than a few instances, quit their jobs in order to participate. While the syndicate takes care of your living expenses during the summer, everyone who competes incurs a financial sacrifice but no one who competes seems to mind.

Harold S. Vanderbilt—Skipper of Enterprise 1930; Rainbow 1934, and Ranger 1937

In reviewing the America's Cup skippers I have known over the past fifty years, one has to start with Harold S. Vanderbilt, known to his intimates as Mike. He is the only three-time winner of the Cup, as skipper of *Enterprise* in 1930, *Rainbow* in 1934, and *Ranger* in 1937. It was not too easy to become intimate with Mike. He had a brilliant mind, as proven by his prowess in bridge and his business accumen. He was socially prominent and supremely confident to the point of being overbearing. When I first knew him as a teenager I thought of him with a mixture of awe and fear. When we served together on the Appeals Committee and Racing Rules Committee of the North American Yacht Racing Union in later years, the fear vanished but the awe remained. His mind was razor sharp and the power of his conviction so strong that, even if you thought he was wrong, you sure as hell thought twice before disagreeing. And even on the rare occasions when he was wrong, it was tough to convince him.

As an America's Cup skipper, however, he was not hard to sail with. He ran his yachts like a business. Everyone knew who was boss but he delegated authority and seldom countermanded a decision of his afterguard. Mike was not a good small boat sailor, but J-boats were anything but small. He showed great judgment in the early decisions so necessary to make such a complicated venture gel and come together at the time of the final trials. He was a great student of the weather and seldom had the wrong sail up and seldom caught on the wrong side of a wind shift. He was also a psychologist, as witness the fact that he always removed the mainsail from the boom each evening even though he was going to race the next day and the main already bent was probably the right one for the next day's weather. J-boat mains weighed over a ton, and it was a backbreaking and time-consuming job to unbend one and bend another, but Mike was smart enough to realize that if a main was already in place in the morning there was the danger, human nature being what it is, to conclude that maybe it would be okay for the expected weather. All mains therefore were put ashore each night so that his judgment of which would be right for the next day would not be colored by which was easier to get at.

He was an innovator too, being the first to develop the timed start, known forevermore as the Vanderbilt start. To illustrate: Knowing it took 40 seconds to jibe a J-boat and reverse course 180°, and assuming you were on the line and reaching away from it with 5 minutes to go, when

Mike Vanderbilt at **Ranger**'s *wheel, surrounded by his afterguard Rod Stephens, Olin Stephens, Lene Bliss, Mike's wife Gertie and Artie Knapp.*

should you jibe to head back? In this instance, the formula would read $\frac{5'+40''}{2} = 2'30'' + 20''$ or 2 minutes 50 seconds being the amount of time *remaining* at which you should commence your jibe to return to the line. For years keen skippers had been doing something similar, but Mike was the first to reduce it to a mathematical formula, which is one reason why his starts were superb. He was smart enough to realize that the formula had to be modified in the event of current, or if he was blanketed or expected to be blanketed either leaving or returning to the line, but having the formula to rely on gave great confidence when returning to the line at eleven knots. In the absence of variables, if the formula said you were not going to be early, you were not early, and this made for gutsy starts with full headway.

Mike was a superb helmsman of J-boats in a strong breeze. He could sense when she was in the groove, not by looking at the sails, but by a combination of feel and by looking at the leeward rail to ensure heel angle was not excessive. Conversely he had a poor feel sailing to windward in light air, tending to drive too much, thus building too much speed but not getting to the windward mark as fast as if he had pointed higher at reduced speed. But he was smart enough to recognize this weakness and that is why others, Sherman Hoyt in 1930 on *Enterprise* and in 1934 on *Rainbow* and Olin Stephens in 1937 on *Ranger,* were the windward helmsmen in light air.

Mike's other great attribute was a mastery of the racing rules and a ruthlessness in using them. This led to some unpleasantness (see chapter eight on famous protests) but it helped him win races.

Two of the three times Mike Vanderbilt defended the Cup, it might well have gone overseas if he had not been in the picture. In 1930 he won in *Enterprise* but it is likely that any one of the four American boats of that year could have beaten *Shamrock V.* In 1934, however, *Endeavour* was certainly a faster boat than *Rainbow* and without Mike's key decisions I feel *Endeavour* would have won (see chapter ten). In 1937 *Ranger* was a super boat and clearly superior to *Endeavour II.* But had it not been for Mike recognizing that unless a new defender was built we would lose the Cup, lose it we surely would have. Remember, those were recession years and the syndicate Mike tried to organize to pay for a new defender never got off the ground. Mike was, of course, a wealthy man but when other wealthy men were keeping their hands in their pockets, he financed *Ranger* virtually singlehandedly. He did so in realization that our existing J-boats were not up to the job of beating *Endeavour II* and for anyone bitten with America's Cup Fever no sacrifice was too much to ensure that the Cup stayed here.

*Charles Francis Adams, the first amateur skipper to defend the cup (*Resolute, 1920*), came within one foot of defending in* Yankee *when she lost the final trial race* Rainbow. *Charlie was a spry 68 at the time and would have been the oldest skipper to defend.*

Charles Francis Adams: Skipper of Resolute 1920 and *Yankee* 1934

Many of the skippers Mike raced against in the J-boat era were better all-around sailors and would have beaten him in smaller boats where it is more of a one-man show, with organization assuming less importance.

One such was Charles Francis Adams. Charlie Adams came from the illustrious Adams family. Two of his direct forebears were Presidents of the United States and Charlie himself was a Secretary of the Navy. He could sail anything well and was the first amateur skipper to win the Cup as skipper of *Resolute* in 1920 against *Shamrock IV*. In 1934 in his sixty-eighth year he beat Mike Vanderbilt's *Rainbow* in their first ten head-to-head races.

Rainbow did win the last two races prior to the final selection trials, but as Mike Vanderbilt wrote in *On the Winds' Highway:* "We were in desperate straits when the trial races began."

When *Yankee* won the first race against *Rainbow* in the final trials by over six minutes, the desperate straits looked even more desperate.

Chapter four entitled "Why the Early Leader Often Loses" describes how *Rainbow* won the next four races to gain selection. She won the final race by a split second—so close that no one on either boat knew who had won. When Charlie Adams, that strong, silent and apparently imperturbable man learned that *Yankee* had lost and that *Rainbow* was to be the defender he broke down and cried—not the only time this has happened to losers of close matches. America's Cup Fever will bring men back to try again, will leave winners with a high they have never felt before, but can leave losers with long-lasting scars. I saw tears running down the cheeks of more than one member of *Intrepid*'s crew in 1974 when, after being tied entering the last race against *Courageous,* they lost in weather they had expected to win in. Others like Bill Cox in *American Eagle,* 1964, and Artie Knapp in *Weatherly* in 1958, while outwardly calm after being eliminated, went through a long period of being withdrawn and lacking their usual bounce. The competition extends over so many months that when you get the axe, especially after you smelled victory, it takes a long time to recover one's equilibrium. I know of no one who has ever suffered a nervous breakdown after a Cup campaign, but there have been some near misses. It is not a game for the faint of heart.

George Nichols—1930

With rare exceptions I will portray only the skippers who actually raced for the Cup in the match itself, not those many fine sailors who failed to survive the trials. One such exception who nearly went all the way was George Nichols, skipper of *Weetamoe* in 1930. You have already met him through a boy's eyes in chapter one, but allow me to expand a bit. George was a gentleman in the finest sense as well as the narrow sense of being in the social register. He epitomized the term yachtsman, looking and dressing

George Nichols, skipper of Weetamoe *in 1930. Better sailors have raced for the Cup, but no finer or kinder men.*

the part. His paid crew of Scandinavians revered him. His afterguard considered him a great person and gave him high marks for organizing a campaign. Their only complaint was the fact that he did not always delegate responsibility or rely on their advice. But the real rub was that he simply was not a very good helmsman. He knew the game from A to Z but was not adept in keeping *Weetamoe* in the groove.

I saw this weakness firsthand when I crewed for George Nichols in the six-meter *Goose* when we won the Scandinavian Gold Cup in three straight races. Counting the selection trials, I raced on *Goose* in thirty races that summer of 1938 and with George Nichols as skipper we won every race.

It would seem, therefore, that he was pretty hot stuff in a boat. Of course he was good, but far from great. We were usually behind at the start, and all too frequently *Goose* was either being driven too hard or pinched. We won because we had a super boat, far faster than her competitors, and when George had her in the groove we walked away from the competition.

After losing the trials to *Enterprise,* George Nichols told her designer Clinton Crane: "Clinton, it is all my fault. The boat was better, but I let you down." I believe he was right. But this remark at the moment of defeat also is a measure of the man. Better sailors than George Nichols have raced for the America's Cup but no better men.

In the modern era a syndicate would probably have switched skippers when *Weetamoe* began to lose. That simply was not done in those days. Had it been, my dad would have been the logical choice. Yes, I am prejudiced, but I also know he was a superb helmsman and an instinctively great sailor. I am confident that in his hands *Weetamoe* would have won.

In respect to my dad's memory, let me emphasize that he *never* told me this, and it never crossed his mind the he would be given *Weetamoe*'s wheel. He never complained about George, but in describing to me how certain races were lost, I knew he was hurting inside. One race was lost by over-standing the mark, and it happened in an odd way. Dad had the finest eyesight of any sailor I know and could see a buoy or a wind shift sooner than anyone. On the day in question, he spotted the tug marking the weather mark and told both the navigator and the skipper that they could tack and fetch it. Unfortunately, there was another vessel which looked like a tug closer than the one standing by the mark. Dad assumed that every-one could see the real mark, but none of them could and they assumed he was referring to the other vessel which indeed they could not fetch. Hence, they overruled him despite his insistence that they could fetch. By the time he realized they saw only the nearer boat and pointed out that he sure as hell did see the mark further upwind, *Weetamoe* was already well past the lay line. Dad blamed himself, not the others, for this breakdown in communication, but if he had been skipper they would have tacked in time and would have retained the lead they had at the time. Instead, it developed into a damaging loss to *Enterprise.*

Ernet Heard, the last of a now extinct breed—the professional racing skipper. He sailed Shamrock V *against* Enterprise *in 1930.*

Ernet Heard—Skipper of Shamrock V *1930*

Ernet Heard was the last of a breed—the professional skipper. Until Charles Francis Adams sailed *Resolute* to victory in 1920 the skipper of defenders and challengers alike were professionals. For many years there had been many good amateur skippers but none of them sailed the really big boats. Perhaps it took so much time to campaign a big boat and to train her crew (which in those days were professional too) that the amateurs couldn't get off from work long enough to do the job. Perhaps the big boats cost so much even in those days that only a few men of enormous wealth could afford them. Being wealthy or a smart businessman doesn't guarantee that you're also a hot sailor. It could be that the owners, knowing they were not up to the job, preferred a professional skipper rather than having to admit that some other amateur was better than they, but then it may have just been bowing to the custom of the days.

I never knew Ernet Heard, though I do remember seeing him—a rugged no-nonsense sort of man, yet with a pleasant demeanor. In the 1930 match he sailed *Shamrock V* competently but was done in by two things. He was up against that master strategist and fine big boat sailor, Mike Vanderbilt. He was also in the hopeless position of sailing a slower boat—a faster boat makes anyone look smart and a slower one makes the best of us look dumb. Heard might have been more aggressive, but even if he had, it wouldn't have done him any good. As it was, I hope he got satisfaction from sailing for the Cup even though his cause was hopeless.

Tom Sopwith—Skipper of the British Challengers Endeavour *1934 and* Endeavour II *1937*

I met Tom Sopwith but I never did know him. I will break my rule about reporting only on people I really knew for two reasons. First, he came closer in *Endeavour* to lifting the Cup in 1934 than anyone ever before or since, and second, I have talked to people who know him well, as recently as 1978. He is obviously a brilliant man, not only as proven by his great success in the aircraft business but in the way he organized *Endeavour.* He also sailed her with a fine touch and with faultless tactics until his colossal error in the third race when an unnecessary tack cost *Endeavour* her third straight win and instead made the score 2–1.

That's one way *Endeavour* lost. She also lost the America's Cup through Sopwith's determination to stand on principle and not bow to pressure he considered unwarranted. Shortly before *Endeavour* left England for America her professional crew struck for higher wages. They probably assumed that they had Sopwith where they wanted him since without them the whole challenge would have to be aborted. But Sopwith felt the wages were eminently fair, considered the demands blackmail, and refused to give in.

Tom Sopwith at Endeavour's *wheel in 1934 came the closest of any challenger to winning the cup, taking the first two races from* Rainbow. *He sailed even better three years later but* Endeavour II *was no match for* Ranger.

Instead, he fired them all and recruited a crew of amateur sailors. The amateurs were excellent but not only did they have insufficient time to train and become a well-oiled machine, but there was not time to develop the callouses required to cope with handling the lines efficiently. *Endeavour's* crew quite literally had bleeding hands before the series was over, and this might have been a real factor in some of their slow sail handling.

In 1937, with a well-trained crew, Sopwith sailed *Endeavour II* superbly, but her cause was hopeless against *Ranger,* the super boat of all America's Cup matches. Had *Endeavour* been as well sailed in 1934 as *Endeavour II* was in 1937, the Cup would surely have gone overseas.

A friend of mine talked to Tom Sopwith in 1978, found him in fine spirits and remembering his two unsuccessful challenges as one of the great experiences of his life—remarkable for one who came so close yet lost and who was involved in bitter protests which were decided against him (see chapter eight).

Briggs Cunningham—Skipper of Columbia 1958

Since the rebirth of America's Cup racing in Twelve Meters, the successful skippers have all had brilliant records in small boats and have made their marks not only in open classes but also in one-design competition. Briggs Cunningham is a quiet man, an unassuming man, but a fierce competitor. He raced sports cars on the European circuit and competed at Le Mans not with a Ferrari, a Porsche, or a Maserati, but with a Cunningham! She was a great car but not quite up to the European cars which had been engineered for road racing for generations. But this effort epitomizes Briggs's delight in a stern challenge.

In sailing he had great success in the 1930s in a series of Six Meters, and in 1947 I had the pleasure of crewing for him in *Goose* when we once again won the Scandinavian Gold Cup. By that time *Goose* was no longer the super boat she was in 1938. In fact, some of the newer designs were faster. But Briggs got good starts, sailed an error-free series, and got the most out of the old girl.

His was always the boat to beat in the Atlantic class, winning several national championships in an era when Atlantics were a highly competitive class.

Briggs is not a flamboyant sailor nor a brilliant one. He can best be characterized as a solid sailor and a very good one who waits for other flashier sailors to make mistakes. His boats are always in superb working order and a breakdown is almost unheard of. He keeps a notebook of things to be done to sails or gear, and this preventive maintenance pays off not only in avoiding breakdowns but in building boat speed.

Briggs is also modest. When *Vim* was beating *Columbia* in a number of trial races it was Briggs's idea to let the famed sailor Corny Shields take a crack at her helm. But Corny, good as he is, got no more out of *Columbia* and when

Briggs Cunningham, the likeable, modest skipper of Columbia *in 1958. Great attention to detail develops the full potential from the boats he sails.*

Briggs resumed the role of skipper he brought her home. When one realizes that he was up against the brilliant Bus Mosbacher in *Vim* and that great sailor Artie Knapp sailing *Weatherly*, Briggs's solid performance is even more noteworthy. *Columbia* competed in three more campaigns under other skippers but never again won, while *Weatherly* became the successful defender in 1962. Briggs may not rank with the best Cup skippers but he is very little behind them and, in my view, underrated except by those who have sailed with or against him.

Bus Mosbacher is no one to fool with on the race course.

Bus Mosbacher—Skipper of Vim *1958,* Weatherly *1962,* Intrepid *1967*

Bus Mosbacher gets my vote as the best America's Cup skipper. He learned the game in Atlantics in the 1930s and in the International One-Design class immediately after World War II when it was in its heyday and populated by such sailing greats as Corny Shields, Bill Cox, Artie Knapp, George Hinman, and others. Bus didn't win each year, but he did emerge as the cream of a tough crop. He sailed dinghies well when at Dartmouth, he won the Mallory Cup and before entering Twelve Meter competition in 1958 had established himself as one of the country's top-ranking small boat sailors.

When he signed aboard the twenty-year-old *Vim* for the 1958 campaign, it was not clear whether or not he was skipper. It did not take long for Bus's brilliance to be recognized, however, and he soon had the wheel. *Vim* was still a good Twelve but in anyone else's hands would not have been a contender against the newer boats. Bus kept her in there right through to the very end of the final trials simply by more aggressive, sharper sailing. He was especially good at starts and devised what were then new tactics of blocking his opponent from getting back to the line on time. His helmsmanship was superb and *Vim* was always in the groove.

Coupled with an instinctive feel and innovative and sound tactics, Bus had the same organizational ability of Mike Vanderbilt. Things seldom went awry on any of his Twelves. You had to beat them and not count on either breakdowns or mistakes to let you through. One rare exception was the second Cup race in 1962 against *Gretel* when *Weatherly* broke her spinnaker pole when the guy was not snagged up soon enough and *Gretel* went on to win. You can bet *Weatherly*'s crew heard about it that night. Bus was tough. He drilled his crew harder than anyone and there was never any doubt as to who was boss. One night a key crew member went out on the town and missed curfew. Despite the fact that *Weatherly* was in the midst of a key set of trial races, the recalcitrant was beached for the next two races. Neither he nor any others were late thereafter.

While Bus was tough he was also fair, and I doubt if any skipper had a more loyal crew.

I found out firsthand how adept he was at starts. After we had been selected to defend the Cup in *Constellation* in 1964 and prior to the match, I invited Bus to come to Newport and practice starts against us. Bus had not raced Twelves for a couple of years, but he brought some of his old crew with him, hopped into our trial horse and proceeded to beat me at the start more often than not. His sense of timing was impeccable, as was his proclivity for handling Twelves like a dinghy, maneuvering within a few feet of us with a daring based on keen judgment of both distance and how fast he could maneuver to clear our stern, jibe inside us, or otherwise give us grief. Yes, we won some starts, something I have always felt I was good at, but Bus won more.

His keen sailing was instrumental in winning the right to defend in *Weatherly* in 1962 as well as in retaining the Cup against *Gretel.* *Weatherly* was improved with hull and rig modifications after her unsuccessful bid in 1958. Still she was no super boat and *Nefertiti,* our only new boat that year, was only good in a breeze. We were vulnerable against *Gretel,* a boat most observers felt was a faster Twelve. *Weatherly* lost one race, another was a real squeaker, but superior handling and tactics brought *Weatherly* home.

In 1967, sailing *Intrepid* against *Dame Pattie,* Bus had it easy. *Intrepid* lost only one trial race all summer, caused by a navigational error in a preliminary race in June—a loss which still rankles Bus. In the match it was no contest. *Dame Pattie* was not the dog many people thought. It was just that *Intrepid* was a super boat, just as *Ranger* had been thirty years before, and in the hands of Bus and his crew she was virtually unbeatable.

Graham Mann—Skipper of the British Challenger Sceptre *1958*

I have little to say about Graham, partly because although I met him in 1958 I never got to know him well. But the pervading reason is the fact that *Sceptre* was so badly outclassed by *Columbia* that it was impossible to get much of a reading on him. Graham did get adequate starts, was tactically sound, and appeared to have *Sceptre* on the wind and in as good a groove as was capable. After losing in light air, the British kept saying "Just wait for a breeze." When the breeze did come, *Columbia* annihilated her. No one could have won in *Sceptre,* not only because her hull was slow, particularly in a seaway, but also because her sails appeared inferior. They also insisted on using huge spinnakers, despite the lesson which could have been learned from our trials to the effect that small chutes were faster, especially in light air. The British were stubborn (stupid might have been a better word) and kept using huge spinnakers, the lighter the air, the larger the chute. Although it sounds like that would work, the big chutes collapsed more, lifted less, and were invariably slower. *Sceptre's* campaign seemed to lack intensity; they seemed more intent in proving the British adage: "It matters not whether you win or lose—it's how you play the game." Mann lost big but he was a fine gent, much liked by all, especially *Columbia's* crew which felt

Graham Mann, shown at Sceptre's *wheel in 1958—one of a long line of genial Englishmen who had "a go" at the Cup in outclassed boats.*

winning was pretty darned important. I'm being too hard on Mann, except for his stubbornness in not using smaller spinnakers. His cause was hopeless no matter what he did. He gets full marks for the seamanlike way his crew jury-repaired a broken main boom in the last race and carried on to the finish, losing little in the process. They were gracious losers.

Jock Sturrock (left) won one race in Gretel *against Bus Mosbacher who sailed* Weatherly. *Bus on* Vim *(1958),* Weatherly *(1962) and* Intrepid *(1967) impressed me as the best of all the fine skippers who defended the cup. Jock had the misfortune of meeting him twice, the second time in 1967 sailing an outclassed* Dame Pattie *against* Intrepid. *Bus's genial shoreside manner changes into a bucko skipper (right).*

Jock Sturrock—Skipper of the Australian Challengers Gretel *1962 and* Dame Pattie *1967*

One of the best liked skippers ever to challenge for the Cup was Jock Sturrock. He is a straightforward, hard-working man with a fine sense of humor and the belief that yacht racing, even when or perhaps especially when, racing for the America's Cup should be fun. He and his crew captivated Newport with their good humor, their productivity for drinking beer after and between races accompanied by much loud (and surprisingly good) singing of "Waltzing Matilda" and other more earthy songs. They discovered a little waterfront restaurant called The Black Pearl and made it their evening headquarters and in the process put it on the map as the "in" place to be. The Black Pearl has since been enlarged, but ever since the Aussies put it on the map it is perpetually jammed. And Jock and his crew knew how to sail. Even though pitted against Bus Mosbacher, in each challenge he got good starts. Their sail handling and general crew work was good, and in the case of *Gretel* in 1962 they came very close to lifting the Cup. Their syndicate head Frank Packer didn't help the cause by switching the navigator on the eve of the first race, nor did he help by keeping Jock up in the air as to whether he would remain as skipper. A navigational lapse might have cost *Gretel* the first race. She won the second, and in another race lost by a scant twenty-six seconds. *Gretel* was surely faster then *Weatherly* in a breeze and was helped by having the first cross-connected coffee grinders, allowing four men to grind the genoa home instead of two for the Americans, a great help in heavy weather tacking duels. Had it been a windy series we would almost certainly have lost in the 1962 match, but it blew hard on only one day.

In light air *Gretel* and *Weatherly* seemed evenly matched. The difference was slightly better sail selection and an absence of tactical errors by Bus and his *Weatherly* crew. Still Jock sailed well and hard. He was there to win and came closer than the 4–1 score would indicate.

In 1967 sailing *Dame Pattie* against *Intrepid* it was no contest but only because *Intrepid* was so outstanding. *Dame Pattie* was a pretty good Twelve, especially in light air. After their first challenge the Aussies apparently decided that designing a light air Twelve was the way to win and got crossed up when it blew stronger than in 1962. But even in light going *Intrepid* was faster and in a breeze it was no contest. As is often the case with an outclassed boat, Jock didn't seem to sail with the same fire as he had five years earlier. He suspected before the series and had it confirmed in the first race that *Dame Pattie* was the slower boat. It was surprising, therefore, that Jock didn't try aggressive starts. Sure, it might not have worked but his only hope of beating *Intrepid* was to smother her at the start, yet he seemed content with getting clear air starts, a hopeless tactic against *Intrepid.* Other than that he sailed well in a hopeless cause.

Eric Ridder—Skipper of Constellation *1964*

Most books and articles on the America's Cup record that I was skipper of *Constellation* in 1964. Not so. Eric Ridder was. It's true that in the final trials and in the match itself I not only was helmsman but also called the shots, with Eric deferring to me should we be in disagreement. Still Eric retained the title of skipper. After all, he was a major contributor to the syndicate and had worked for many months getting *Constellation* and her crew organized. When the syndicate managers decided to let me sail the boat, they asked if Eric could remain as skipper although I was to have full authority, especially from the sounding of the ten minute gun until the finish. I demurred at first because I felt it might be difficult to assume the role of skipper without being acknowledged as same. But once assured by Eric that I was to have a free hand, I agreed. Here I am talking about myself when we are really talking about Eric but we became so intertwined that it's impossible not to.

Eric is a good sailor, with an Olympic gold medal to his credit in the Six Meter class. He also has had a fine record in ocean racing. His other great attribute was a flair for organizing the boat and ensuring all was in readiness. He was calm and bore up well under the pressures of a Cup campaign. Moreover, he is a perfect gentleman and a real fine guy. What's more, on the race course he has a complete grasp of match race tactics.

He had several shortcomings, however, which proved to be fatal. First, he didn't have the sense of timing or of distance to get good starts. Second, he had great trouble keeping *Constellation* in the groove and going her best when on the wind. Often we were either pinching or driving too much and very seldom just right. In these regards he reminds me of George Nichols. Eric also was stubborn in sticking to systems he believed in, even when all the evidence indicated they were wanting. For example, he had developed an intricate jibing method with lines leading into the end of the pole to cam cleats. The cams often slipped and we kept botching our jibes; we even lost a couple of early races because of the system before a near mutiny on the foredeck persuaded Eric to switch to the tried and proven *Vim* jibing method.

Eric sailed *Constellation* in the June and July trials and amazed a record of seven wins and eight losses, including five losses against *American Eagle* which had a record of fourteen wins and no losses for the same period.

It is a matter of record (and I hope not to be construed as boasting on my part) that once Eric turned *Constellation* over to me her record for the rest of the summer was thirteen wins and three losses, with ten of the wins coming against *American Eagle.*

Eric demonstrated the fact that even in a fast boat it's not enough to be just a good sailor to win in America's Cup competition. You've got to be better than good. But he remained a great guy to the very end, never showing any sour grapes or envy when I managed to turn *Constellation* into a winner. When we approached the finish line of the final America's Cup race, I asked Eric to take the wheel. He refused and refused even to share the wheel with me as we crossed the line. That's the kind of guy he is.

Bob Bavier—Helmsman of Constellation *1964, Skipper of Courageous 1974*

This is a tough one. How do you analyze yourself without sounding like a pompous ass or a shrinking violet? But since I was involved in two successful Cup campaigns an attempt must be made. In his foreword to my book *A View from the Cockpit* Peter Scott describes me as a modest man. I'll try to not prove him wrong and at the same time present an objective appraisal.

I've raced small boats ever since I was eleven years old, with good success in keen classes. I've also done a great deal of ocean racing. Probably my strongest attribute is the ability to steer a boat fast on all points of sailing, coupled with a good sense of the special tactics of downwind sailing. In his foreword to my book, *A View from the Cockpit,* Peter wrote: "The point should not be missed that *Constellation* was sailed with superlative skill by a great natural Twelve Meter helmsman—probably the best in the world."

That bit of hyperbole should be taken in context as coming from someone I had beaten decisively and hence perhaps not completely objective or accurate. But Peter is right on the natural part. I'm not a particularly scientific sailor but do have a good touch and an instinctive feel when a boat is going her best and the ability to keep her there, as well as a good knowledge of tactics.

In 1964 I was loose. When I took over, *Constellation* had never beaten our main adversary *American Eagle.* Hence I had nothing to lose and could be relaxed. I also had the benefit of feeling that *Constellation* was a shade faster than *American Eagle* and a lot faster than the other contenders, knowledge which allowed me to sail *Constellation* conservatively, concentrating on getting the maximum speed out of her with the assurance that if I didn't hack it this would be enough to see us through. It worked, as witness our thirteen win three loss record thereafter, one loss occurring when we were dismasted. Since we had never beaten *Eagle* before it is evident that *Constellation*'s slightly better boat speed wasn't the full answer, but it sure helped. As for the match itself against *Sovereign* we won by the greatest margins in America's Cup history but I take little pride in that. A trained monkey could have sailed

Bob Bavier made Constellation *come alive in 1964 but ten years later (below) didn't get the most out of* Courageous.

Constellation to victory over the hopelessly outclassed *Sovereign.*

Ten years later in *Courageous* it was quite a different story. Here we were the preseason favorite and this made for a less relaxed atmosphere. Early races against *Mariner* and *Valiant* to whom we never lost all summer reaffirmed our favorite's role. But when we hooked up against *Intrepid* in the preliminary trials at Newport it was quite a different story. Upwind we were definitely slower than *Intrepid,* primarily because our experimental Kevlar main was a dog. Downwind we had a decided edge, however, partly because of better spinnakers, partly I feel because we sailed better. We had an even record against *Intrepid* in June but each win was such a struggle that this didn't build my confidence.

In all honesty I think I sailed *Courageous* very well in June. We shared starting honors against *Intrepid,* we won the tacking duels and we were superior on the downwind legs. Inferior boat speed did us in to windward.

The syndicate, however, was not pleased and between the June and July trials insisted we spend hours sailing upwind checking against our computer to determine whether I was getting the most out of her. We also practiced tacking, with the computer being used as a gauge to determine the most efficient tacking speed. In retrospect I should have insisted on spending more time perfecting our sails. In July we started losing the tacking duels. Our windward speed had improved a trifle but was still inferior to *Intrepid.* Downwind they had closed the gap to where there was little to choose. Worst of all, I started losing the majority of the starts against *Intrepid.* Strangely I won most of the starts against Ted Turner in *Mariner.* Ted in turn edged Gerry Driscoll who was sailing *Intrepid,* yet I was losing the starts to Gerry. Obviously I was getting tight and not sailing as well as I should against our main rival.

In between the July trials and the selection trials of August we got new sails. The only rub was that we didn't have enough time to determine which sails were best in the various wind ranges. When the final trials began, it was apparent at once that *Courageous* was much improved and for the first time a shade faster upwind. Not so her skipper. I had been fed so much advice that I was no longer sailing instinctively but rather trying to follow the advice, some of which I didn't believe in. Result—I was sailing pretty poorly. I kept beating Turner at the starts, while losing most of the starts to Driscoll. The syndicate quite wisely directed me to let Ted Hood sail upwind after the start, with me sailing downwind. Then, after *Mariner* and *Valiant* had been eliminated, Dennis Conner came aboard as starting helmsman, Ted sailed upwind, and I sailed downwind. It could have been a good combination, but by this time I had lost so much confidence that I wasn't making sound decisions nor very forceful ones. You have to have one overall boss on a boat and in effect we had three, with me being the titular boss but not acting as such. Hence we delayed in our decisions, each deferring to the other. Still, with this combination we managed a 4–4 record against *Intrepid.* Everyone knew that the next boat to win a race would be selected, and the syndicate felt that they had to make a decisive move to improve our chances. They voted to kick me off, promote Ted Hood to skipper, and retain Dennis as starting helmsman and tactician.

I have no quarrel with the decision. I wasn't sailing well, I was not sufficiently forceful and Ted was better than I. Under Ted's leadership *Courageous* did win the next race and that gave her the selection. Maybe I could have won it, maybe not, but the decision was a sound one. I quarrel only with the way I got the word, being notified as I was walking down the dock to step aboard as skipper for the climactic race and being told that I was no longer wanted. Had we discussed the situation the evening before (as the public was led to believe), I am sure I would have agreed and then it would have been a joint decision by me and the syndicate to make what was a logical move. But it was not discussed! I was simply told I was beached, which was a tough way to end three months of racing, with but one race to go.

My biggest mistake, I feel, was in not insisting on doing things my own instinctive way and also in not insisting that we get new sails before the July trials. I requested them, but when told I should wait till August, I backed down and went along.

So how do you rate Bob Bavier as an America's Cup skipper? Probably pretty high marks for 1964, pretty low ones for 1974. I still feel that doing things my own way I could have pulled it off in 1974, but I allowed myself to be coerced into doing it other people's way instead, with disastrous results. I made one other mistake. When things were so tight in the final trials, I should have taken myself off the boat instead of having to be kicked off. What is that saying about aging prize fighters being the last to recognize or to admit that they are over the hill and not the hot stuff they still consider themselves to be?

Peter Scott—Skipper of the British Challenger Sovereign *1964*

Peter Scott, now Sir Peter Scott, is as close to being a renaissance man as anyone I know. He excels at anything he does. His father, Robert Falcon Scott, was the noted explorer who reached the South Pole in 1912, only to die from hunger and cold on the return to their headquarters on Ross Island.

Peter inherited his father's adventuresome spirit and love of a stern challenge as well as a fierce determination to excel.

And excel he does. He took up airplane soaring in middle age and within a few years was European champion. He became a television commentator and soon had one of Britain's leading programs. He is a superlative painter, specializing in depicting waterfowl (Canada geese are his favorite subject) in their natural habitat but also was a good enough portrait painter to be commissioned to do a portrait of the Queen. He is one of the world's leading ornithologists and now head of the Wildfowl Trust at Slimbridge, England. In recent years he has gotten interest in scuba diving and snorkeling and travels worldwide on underwater expeditions recording what he has seen through magnificent photos. He is a polished and successful author.

He was for a number of years president of the International Yacht Racing Union and responsible in making it international in fact as well as in name. The skill with which he conducts a stormy meeting, keeps it on course, and gains decisions from widely diverse factions has to be seen to be believed.

And in yacht racing like anything else he was a past master, winning an Olympic Medal in his youth and the famed Prince of Wales Cup for the International 14 class when it was in its heyday.

The quest for the America's Cup is the very sort of challenge Peter would revel in. And it turned out to be one of the few challenges that he failed to win. In his foreword to *A View From The Cockpit* he writes: "To me the words 'America's Cup' mean the most publicized and spectacular failure of my life." He was right but the failure was due to the boat and the sails, not the way he sailed her. Peter did almost all anyone could hope to, given the tools he had to work with. First of all, his sails were no match for ours. Second, her hull shape was such as to slow her and induce hobbyhorsing in a seaway. I sailed *Sovereign* in one race against *Constellation* two years later (1966) in Marseilles and won with her. But, and it's an enormous but, *Sovereign* was then equipped with new Hood sails and the water was smooth. When seas built up, *Constellation* gained like crazy. And at Newport in 1964 there was always a sea caused both by the wash from the spectator craft and the wind.

Peter seemed not too tough to beat at the start in the two races we were trying to win the start. In the other two we went just for clear air since we knew we had such an edge in speed we could lose only through a foul or perhaps a severe deficit at the start. Peter should have been more aggressive at starts, and he and his crew were stubborn in flying too large a spinnaker for the bumpy conditions. But in other respects he sailed as well as could be expected. In a match race it is very difficult to look smart and sharp with a vastly slower boat.

Peter was his charming, witty self at the press conferences after each race. He is not typically British in that he came to win, not just to play the game, but he knew how to lose with dignity.

He had the following to say about losing in his foreword to my book:

> So we were beaten—badly beaten—a combination which failed
> miserably to compete with a superior combination, but after all
> we had done our best. The series had been conducted without a

single unhappy incident or protest. Much had been learned about Twelve Meters, their design, their sails, their handling. New friendships had been made and old ones confirmed. Even as we sailed back into Newport Harbor after the last race of the Cup series I knew that for me the effort had been worthwhile. Tony Boyden, *Sovereign*'s owner, has told me that he felt the same, even on that last bitter evening.

To my knowledge, Peter Scott has never raced a boat since, but only because he has sought other worlds to conquer and also because he is too smart to race for the Cup again with inferior tools. But sixteen years later Tony Boyden is backing a new British challenge with a boat he hopes will be a sharp tool. For some America's Cup fever never dies—it just goes dormant.

Bill Ficker—Skipper of Intrepid *1970*

Bill Ficker looks like Mr. Clean but sails a lot smarter. An architect by profession, he brought a scientific analytical mind to Cup sailing, and pitted against *Gretel II* it is lucky he did. Bill is an ex-Star Class world champion, proof positive of his small boat prowess. But he's particularly adept at organizing a larger boat like a Twelve. Bill worked efficiently in training his crew and perfecting the boat and sails and in the actual races delegated much authority to his tactician Steve Van Dyke and his navigator Peter Wilson. The tactics were left largely in their hands, with Bill reserving a veto power which he seldom exercised. This allowed him to concentrate on steering—a good thing because *Intrepid* was not an easy boat to sail, especially in light air. She had been modified by Britton Chance after her triumph in 1967, and most knowledgeable yachtsmen feel she was slowed in the process. Her keel was shortened and her displacement increased. In a breeze she was probably faster than before but in light air was sluggish, accelerating slowly after tacks and making excessive leeway until she regained headway.

The other new American boats *Valiant* and *Heritage* had similar weak-

Bill Ficker looks like Mr. Clean but sails a whole lot better. Only masterful sailing of Intrepid *in 1970 staved off* Gretel II.

nesses. All three were excessively heavy. The history of boats built to the International Rule had been that the larger and heavier the boat the better the performance. This time all three American designers (Chance on *Intrepid,* Sparkman and Stephens on *Valiant* and Charles Morgan on *Heritage*) had gone too far. They hoped to remain competitive in light air by reducing wetted surface but had gone too far, and all three boats had too great a resemblance to a dinosaur. The handwriting was on the wall when the venerable and over the hill *Weatherly* gave them fits during the trials in light air. The Cup was up for the grabbing and only a superlative job by Ficker and his afterguard kept *Gretel II* from taking it to Australia.

We will get back to Ficker and how he won the 1970 match in chapter ten where we discuss the times the Cup was nearly lost and in chapter eight which covers famous protests. Let it be recorded here, however, that he did one whale of a job.

Jim Hardy—Skipper of the Australian Challenger Gretel II *1970 and* Southern Cross *1974.*

He became known as Gentleman Jim Hardy, and with good reason. No more likable skipper ever challenged for the Cup. He was polite, affable, diplomatic in his statements and fun to be with. Underneath this smooth veneer was a fierce will to win. While he was charming Newport ashore he was out to get us afloat, and he came so very close! Helping him was the fact that he was a fine sailor, with a good touch at the wheel. Had he realized soon enough that in *Gretel II* he had the fastest Twelve of that year in light and moderate air, and had he governed his tactics accordingly, I believe he would have won. He could well have won also if he had known racing rule 42.3 which restricts the rights of a leeward yacht at the starting line after the starting signal. *Gretel II* did win one race and would have won another if Hardy had known this rule but instead he was disqualified.

We will revisit Hardy and learn how he lost in chapters eight and ten. Suffice it to say now that in 1970 he had the tools to win the Cup but despite sailing well he let the greatest prize of all escape his grasp.

In 1974, sailing *Southern Cross* against *Courageous* he was outgunned. Again he sailed well, though not brilliantly. Although no match against Dennis Conner at the starts, in the first two races he was in the fight. He had the lead on the first leg of one of them and could have won if he had not overstood the mark. In the other he had a chance to round the first mark first, and since *Southern Cross* was a fast reaching boat would be expected to hold her lead thereafter. Still *Courageous* was enough faster upwind to make the Australian's cause extremely difficult. In the second race, however, *Cross* lost by little over a minute, though trailing all the way, proof that she was no dog and in fact capable of winning if she outsailed *Courageous.*

After the first two races, Hardy in a desperation move switched sails. The replacement sails were inferior, however, and *Courageous* won big. Again I feel he did not recognize how competitive his boat was. In *Gretel II* against *Intrepid* he had the slightly faster boat. In *Southern Cross* he was very slightly slower than *Courageous* until the sail switching. It would have been far better, I feel, for him to have stuck with the sails which a summer of experience indicated were his best rather than indulging in wishful thinking by trying different ones and thus putting himself completely out of it.

Ted Hood—Skipper of Courageous *1974.*

I have sailed more against and with Ted Hood than any of the other America's Cup skippers, and often I still do not know what he is thinking. He is an extremely quiet and shy man. I have raced with him as navigator on two Newport–Bermuda races, one of which he won. I have raced with him in the SORC. I raced against him in the America's Cup Trials in 1964 when he was skipper of *Nefertiti,* and finally we spent the summer together on *Courageous* when he was my number two before I got bounced. We are

good friends but still I do not feel I know him all that well since he is a very private man.

He lets his sailing and his sailmaking speak for him. He delegates authority almost to an extreme, picking good people to sail with him and then counting on them to do their job. For example, when I was navigating for him in the Bermuda Race, the second day out there was a decision to be made as to whether we should tack. I thought we should, but it was an iffy thing and I really wanted to discuss the options with Ted. I planned to show him on the chart exactly where we were and explain the pros and cons of tacking as I saw it. But I prefaced my remarks by saying I thought we should tack, and Ted never let me explain my reasoning. True, I had raced to Bermuda many times and this was Ted's first, but still I wanted to share the burden of the tack with Ted. He wouldn't sit still for any reasoning and instead hollered to the helmsman: "The navigator says we should tack, so let's go." Thank God, it turned out to be a wise tack; we hit the Gulf Stream at the point of the most favorable current and went on to win. What I am pointing out is that Ted not only trusts you to do a good job, he expects it. When you don't, you don't get chewed out, but later on the error of ommission or commission is discussed quietly but forthrightly.

A passenger sailing for the first time and viewing him operating with a good crew might come to the erroneous conclusion that Ted lacks leadership. Not so. He never says anything unnecessary but when leadership is required he is there to give it. He has an uncanny feel for when a boat is not going her best. On that first Bermuda Race Ted was apparently dozing in his bunk below but propped his head up the companionway and without even looking around asked: "What are you guys doing? Cruising? Get the number one jib on." We had been debating whether we should replace the number two but were not sure. Ted in his bunk *was* sure and as usual he was right.

I do not feel that Ted is a top organizer except for surrounding himself with able people, but he can sure sail a boat. He steers well and has a superb knowledge of tactics. He is only a fair match race starter but not averse to letting someone else start for him (providing that someone is named Dennis Conner or someone else of similar competence). But in the climactic race against *Intrepid* in the final trials of 1974 Ted started himself. It was blowing so hard that Ted probably didn't want Dennis trying any fancy stuff and risking a breakdown. Instead Ted got a conservative start, slightly behind *Intrepid* but on the side of her he wanted to be and with clear air. It was a good start for the conditions and it did the job. I am also sure that Ted felt *Courageous* would be faster in that going and hence a safe clear air start was all that was needed. In that he was right.

While Ted was serving as my tactician on *Courageous,* his reticence in speaking out was a detriment. There were times I would have welcomed far more input. Ted is, I feel, a better skipper than he is a crew or an advisor.

There is another side of Ted's character which needs airing. As everyone knows, he is a superb sailmaker and in the 1964 trials was building sails for all the contenders. He was racing *Nefertiti* against us, but I could swear he spent even more time on our sails, and as recut by him they became even better than the ones he had on his own boat. Ted would come aboard, look at our sails, and even when we thought they were perfect, he would ask for them to go ashore for a bit of recutting. I never questioned Ted on this and seldom even asked what he intended to do with them. They would come back a day later better than ever. Ted is a man you can trust.

In the match against *Southern Cross* he sailed an error-free series, and with his slightly faster boat that was the ball game.

Ted Turner—Skipper of Mariner *1974 and* Courageous *1977*

What do you say about Ted Turner, "the mouth of the South," that has not been chronicled many times over? Roger Vaughn has written two books about him. He has been interviewed by *Playboy* and been featured in *People* magazine as well as all the boating magazines. The press loves him because he is such good copy, quick with one-liners, and never dull. As the flamboyant owner of the Atlanta Braves baseball team and the basketball Atlanta Hawks, he has become known to the general public, not just to yachtsmen. In the long history of the America's Cup no skipper has done more to draw attention to the contest. Now, not only yachtsmen but cab drivers, ball players, rural housewives and, in fact, people of all ages and all walks of life know about the races. They may call it the "American Cup" races, "that sailboat race at Newport," or some outlandish name, but they know about it as never before. And they care! Many misguided yachtsmen want the challenger to win, but the great American public wanted Ted Turner to beat the Australians. He was the people's choice.

Ted reveled in the publicity. He genuinely loves being in the limelight and gets such a charge out of it that it becomes infectious and no one really minds that he is a ham. The fact that his talk is well-laced with humor keeps people from taking offense at most of his outlandish remarks. I remember when we were having a drink together after the first Admiral's Cup Race several years ago at Cowes, England. The German team had won the first race and sailors from many nations were gathered around the bar. Ted announced in a loud voice: "Don't worry about those Germans—they're always fast starters. Remember what happened to them after 1914 and

44

1939?" Even the Germans laughed (but in this instance, they had the last laugh by holding on to win the Admiral's Cup).

Vain, cocky, brash, loud, proud—all these adjectives fit Ted Turner. Less flattering words like crude and rowdy apply occasionally, but even more accurate are such terms as straight, honest, loyal. There is nothing phony about Ted Turner, and, strange as it may seem, he does not have an exalted view of himself. He knows he is a good sailor and will freely admit it, but he also knows and acknowledges when he goofs or when someone else has done a better job, either in sailing or in business. When he wins he is apt to come ashore and announce: "We annihilated them. It was just like Sherman marching through Georgia." When he loses he is apt to say: "I sailed a lousy race." And speaking of business, in his twenties he inherited a family business which was on the verge of bankruptcy and developed it so well that he is now a self-made multimillionaire.

If you are not sure whether Ted Turner likes you, do not ask. If he thinks you are a jerk, he will tell you so. But if he likes you do not expect flattery. He shouts at his crew, often in uncomplimentary fashion, but I know this is just to keep them on their toes. Still, he is not one to sail with if you have got a thin skin. In 1978 I was crewing for Ted on *Tenacious* at Newport week. Handling the main sheet was Wally Stenhouse, a strong, well-conditioned man in his fifties. Wally is a great sailor, having preceded Ted as World Ocean Racing Champion and was doing a good job trimming the main during prestart maneuvering. But not fast enough to suit Ted who hollered to his crew: "Get that geriatric case off the main and find someone who can trim it." Wally did not bat an eye and he still sails with Ted. All of us who have sailed with Ted receive abuse in the heat of battle, but we all realize that it is Ted's way of letting off steam and keeping everyone sharp and that no offense is intended. It is significant that every single crew member who sailed with him on the 1977 defense of the Cup will be with him in 1980, and that everyone who started the 1977 campaign on *Courageous* was there at the end, with no substitutions.

How good a sailor is Ted Turner? If you had asked me that in 1974, I would have said: "Good, but far from great." Sure he had a slow boat then and slow boats tend to make anyone look bad. Still he was not too tough to beat at the start and some of his tactics seemed questionable. But three years later sailing *Courageous* he was outstanding. He clearly outsailed Lowell North and Ted Hood, and that is no small achievement. Not only was he sharp personally but he trained his crew so well that *Courageous* was the best handled of the lot. Ted was quieter in 1977, relying more on his crew rather than trying to direct everything himself, a prior weakness. Gary Jobson on tactics and Robbie Doyle on sail trim were given quite a free hand, thus letting Ted concentrate on steering fast. He almost always had *Courageous* going her best.

Ted Turner is a self-made sailor rather than one born with unusual natural skills. He sailed Lightnings for a number of years before even winning his home club's championship. But hard work and a great deal of sailing in boats of all sizes and types have made him a truly fine sailor. Let there be no mistake—Ted Turner loves sailing, loves the competition, and does more of it than anyone I know. Now that he is on top there is no slackening. He keeps putting it on the line, keeps racing in top competition even though he has no new worlds to conquer. I feel he does it more because he loves racing than he does to keep in the limelight. Having won in *Courageous* as an underdog in 1977 one could expect that he would rest on his laurels. But that is not Turner. He will be back against new boats and improved old ones and it is going to be tough indeed to repeat. Knowing this only makes him more determined to try.

In the 1977 match *Courageous* was up against a tough challenger. If *Australia* had as good jibs, if she had gotten as good starts, and if her tactics had been as sharp, she could have beaten *Courageous*. The apparent easy victory scored by *Courageous* was not due to far better boat speed but instead to the fact that Turner and Company did a better job. They were usually ahead at the start and invariably went the right way thereafter. They often made a loose cover after *Australia*'s initial clearing tack, and each time made a big gain by letting their opponent go the wrong way. Having built a commanding lead, they then sailed conservatively with the margin between the two boats remaining virtually constant. Yes, *Courageous* was a shade faster but just a shade.

I rate Ted Turner close to the top among all America's Cup skippers.

Noel Robbins—Skipper of the Australian Challenger Australia *1977*

While Noel Robbins is a very pleasant chap and a sound sailor, there seemed little to distinguish him. Maybe it was all bottled up within, but he seemed to lack any fierce will to win and, in fact, appeared to expect *Courageous* to win and to accept it. He got decent starts but not the aggressive ones to be expected from a challenger who expects his boat to be slower. He lost a great chance to win the third race. Turner got too far away from the line with several minutes to go. When he started back, Robbins who was nearer the line, instead of tacking on *Courageous*'s wind fell in on her weather beam. *Courageous* from that time on went full out for the line but

Noel Robbins is a thoroughly pleasant chap, perhaps too pleasant to get the aggressive starts Australia *needed to have a chance against* Courageous *in 1977.*

was still twenty-two seconds late, and with a safe leeward on *Australia.* Had Robbins tacked on her wind he could have slowed *Courageous* down enough to win the start by thirty seconds. Had he covered well thereafter he should have been able to stay on top because *Australia* was going well in that race, and after getting behind early lost only two seconds on the last five legs of the course. It was a golden opportunity to capitalize on the one big error made by Turner in the entire series.

Most observers thought the match was a rout. I will admit the outcome seemed inevitable after the first leg of the first race, but I feel that if the crews had switched boats and jibs the Americans still would have won. Match racing can seem far more one-sided than it is if a slightly faster boat is also the better sailed boat. The Aussies should be disappointed with their performance but not discouraged. They came closer to being really in it than most people realize.

Let's Hear It for the Crews

It is axiomatic in yacht racing and certainly true of the America's Cup that the skipper gets the lion's share of the credit for victory and most of the blame for losing. It is not fair either way but that is how the ball bounces. Actually, the skipper is like the quarterback of a football team, certainly a key man but he needs a good line (winch grinders), good ends (foredeck), good backs (the afterguard). Twelve Meters sail with a crew of eleven. J-boats sailed with approximately thirty and the huge sloops like *Reliance,* at the turn of the century, had forty-three on board.

Without a good crew and especially without a good tactician and crew boss or sail trimmer, no skipper has a chance in America's Cup competition.

Most skippers who have sailed for the America's Cup feel they had the best crew ever to sail in the epic event, which is not surprising since they have never had as good a crew before nor ever will again. America's Cup racing has such allure that the finest sailors try out for it, and only the finest of the fine are finally chosen and go all the way to the match itself.

I will let you in on a secret which other Cup skippers will deny but which is true nonetheless—the finest America's Cup crew of all time was the one which sailed *Constellation* to victory in 1964. They were the best not because of being better sailors than many other Cup crews but because of their character. Most crews would have wilted and become discouraged when we went all through the June and July trials, never once beating our main rival *American Eagle.* Not so *Constellation*'s crew. They just worked harder, kept their cool, and sailed better than even they thought they could. And they kept having fun. Their names in alphabetical order: Bob Bavier, Buddy Bombard, Put Brown, Bob Connel, Dick Enersen, Dun Gifford, Dick Goennel, John Handel, Fenny Johnson, Fred Kulicke, Eric Ridder, Larry Scheau, Rod Stephens, Steve Van Dyke. You will note that I have mentioned fourteen names. This includes three alternates who made such a tremendous contribution to our success.

It is too bad that space does not permit describing these sailors and the other great men who have defended and challenged for the America's Cup. Let's talk about just one to represent the hundreds who have sailed so brilliantly. I refer to Rod Stephens who has crewed on three Cup defenders over a period of twenty-seven years: *Ranger* 1937, *Columbia* 1958, and *Constellation* 1964. On *Ranger* his assigned job was rover in charge of the crew and rig. He was tougher and more agile than any of *Ranger's* professional crew and delighted in some snafu aloft which allowed him to climb the rigging hand over hand to fix it before a bosun's chair could be rigged.

On *Constellation* he came aboard late, primarily at my suggestion, when I became helmsman. I wanted someone I could rely on to be a second pair of eyes and as tactician. I also wanted someone who could get that little extra out of the crew, not in effort because they were all putting out to their utmost, but in welding them into a more efficient team. Having crewed with Rod, I knew he was just what we needed. His title was navigator but in actuality he was also my number two, the crew boss, rover, and general expert. His contribution was enormous and a big factor in our turnaround.

Actually, I did not want him as navigator because we had a superb one in Dun Gifford who, because of his ability and affability, was I felt important to our success. There was no one I *wanted* to get rid of to make room for Rod because all were good. But I did want to keep Dun almost above all others and recommended beaching someone else to make way. This was the only matter the syndicate overruled me on, but let it be recorded here and now that the best sailor ever to be replaced on a Cup defender was Dun Gifford. I did, however, get him back on board for the third race against *Sovereign.*

Though Rod's contribution was for more than that as navigator, his innate sense of navigation iced one win against *American Eagle.* We had a narrow lead over *Eagle* a few minutes after the start when we sailed into a pronounced header. As we did Rod scrambled below, made a quick plot on the chart and emerged seconds later with the remark, "You can tack and fetch." "Are you sure?" I asked. When Rod said "yes" that was good enough for me. We tacked away from *Eagle* while on her weather beam. It had never occurred to them that we were at the lay line. It was amusing to see the consternation in their cockpit and to see their navigator rush below. It was a full minute before they matched our tack, a minute thrown away when we fetched ("of course," Rod would say) with fifty yards to spare after sailing on that tack for three and a half miles.

*Rod Stephens kept things working and was an outstanding crew on three defenders—*Ranger *1938,* Columbia *1958 and* Constellation *1964. He never crewed on a losing Cup boat.*

One other thing about Rod which bears telling is the way he feels about boats. A good one is to him not just a conglomeration of wood, steel, aluminum, and dacron but instead something which almost lives and breathes. After a good performance he will pat the boat's topsides and will talk to her like a rider patting a horse after a successful steeplechase. Rod is so caught up in everything that makes a boat go fast, everything that makes her hold together that the boat becomes a part of him and of his thinking. Hence she almost becomes alive. He is not a timid sailor but is a conservative one, knowing how hard a boat should be driven, but stopping just short of driving beyond the brink and perhaps injuring her (or the crew). On ocean racers he is apt to shorten down sooner than others and usually just before the other boats go into a wild broaching act. Rod Stephens is a superlative seaman as well as a superlative sailor. A good man to have on your team! He epitomizes the sort you sail with when racing for the America's Cup.

Chapter III
Match Race Tactics

While it is unlikely that many readers of this book will ever compete in match racing and fewer still in the premier match race of all, an understanding of match racing is essential to a full appreciation of the America's Cup. It's a dog-eat-dog affair where the emphasis must focus on how you can hinder the other boat. Second is a pretty good finish in most races. In a match race second is last and hence both in philosophy and in tactics one's approach must differ from fleet racing.

The start is always important in a yacht race. In match racing it assumes even greater importance. This is particularly true if the two boats are even in speed or if you feel your boat is slower. In a slower boat, getting on top at the start is just about the only realistic way you could hope to win. That's why it is surprising to see slower challengers not sailing aggressively at the start. They have so little to lose by trying. If their aggressive approach backfires and they get clobbered at the start, it means only that they lose by a greater margin than they would have. If the tactics work it gives them a shot at victory.

With two even boats the start is also vital since the early leader has a tremendous edge. Only if you know your boat is faster should you be conservative at the start. Then you should go for a clear air start and not a dramatic one. This is easy to achieve and makes it almost impossible for the slower boat to stay ahead for long. In the first Cup race in 1964 we on *Constellation* were aggressive at the start because we were not sure we were faster. It was fun to win that start. The first race showed us that we were so much faster than *Sovereign* that the only way we could lose was by being beaten badly at the start. Hence we let *Sovereign* have her own way, let her edge us at the start in the next two races, *but in the process* we ensured that we were close behind and had clear air—all we needed to assume the lead within a mile of the start. I got angry, however, when the daily press, in reporting on those races, indicated that "Bavier sure couldn't start as well as Scott, but his boat bailed him out." Hence in the fourth race, much against our advisors' wills, we went after *Sovereign* hard at the ten minute gun and got her into such a position that in trying to beat us across the line they were early. It was, I suppose, a childish reaction on my part, since we knew by then that all we needed was clear air in order to win. But just winning isn't everything. You've got to be proud about how you won, how you sailed, and I knew for an absolute certainty that even if I blew the start completely, was over ahead of the gun or a half dozen lengths dead to leeward of *Sovereign* and dead in the water at the start, we could still catch her. Hence in this instance a conservative start wasn't necessary.

But in watching future America's Cup matches, if in the first race one boat proves faster, don't castigate her skipper if he is edged in all subsequent starts. That great starter Bus Mosbacher had indifferent starts in *Intrepid*'s 1967 match against *Dame Pattie.* He was absolutely right in so doing because everyone knew *Intrepid* was a super boat. The blame should rest on Sturrock's shoulders not Bus's for accepting even starts in a slower boat.

Constellation *is squeezing up under* Sovereign *into a safe leeward position. Note how much flatter* Constellation*'s sails are.*

The fact that he suspected Bus would outmaneuver him if he tried to mix it up is no excuse. *He had to try.*

O.K., we've established the importance of starts in a match race. How do you go about winning the start? There is no single simple answer, but the goal is to so maneuver as to be able to control the other boat's action to your benefit. The circling maneuvers are done in an attempt to get on the other boat's tail and so close that she is unable to tack or jibe without fouling. The trailing boat can thus control the actions of the boat ahead and hopefully keep her from returning to the line on time. When time has run out you can then go for the line and the other boat has no recourse but to follow. Remember, in a match race it matters not at all how late you are at the start provided you are ahead of your adversary.

This tactic will work only if you can block the other boat while maneuvering outside the extremities of the starting line. If within the extremities and to leeward of the line and able to fetch one or both ends, the leading boat, even if blocked from tacking or jibing, can stall and wait until time has nearly run out and then go for it. The trailer still has a slight advantage since he can keep forcing the action, continually trying to prod the leader closer to the line. If he times his start well, he can accelerate sooner, break through, and if all is timed to perfection, can probably either get a safe leeward or choose which end of the line to cross at, with the boat she had been tailing often forced to go for the unfavored end to avoid being blanketed. In short, the tailing position is a good one if you can pull it off— dramatically good if you have lured your adversary beyond the extremities and helpful even if you haven't.

How best to get on the tail? If possible, when you first hook up it is desirable to be on port tack, reaching with full speed and attempt to pass close to leeward of the other boat which is reaching on starboard tack. If he is smart he will try to get to leeward of you, but attempt to forestall this by bearing off yourself. Above all, allow enough time to build maximum boat speed before you meet, even if this means sharpening up on a reach and passing to windward of your adversary, who would now be broad off

Prestart circling wasn't invented by the Twelve Meter skippers. Here the J-boats Rainbow *and* Endeavour *go at it in 1934.*

to get to leeward of you and hence going slow. With your extra speed you might be able to jibe or tack (depending on where he goes) and get on his tail before he can regain speed.

Let's assume, however, that everything has gone well and you do approach on port tack and are reaching to leeward of your opponent on starboard tack. A favorite and excellent maneuver is to head up just as you pass, as if to tack with the assumption that he will jibe in hopes of getting on your tail. After you fake a tack, then bear off and jibe. If he continues to bear off and jibe, when you jibe you are on starboard tack and he on port. Even if no foul ensues he has to think then of avoiding a foul, and has to so maneuver that he can't think of getting on your tail. If he jibes back you will be on his tail. If he attempts to tack clear, it will have to be such a sudden tack that he will lose way and you might again be able to get on his tail.

The first time you get together presents the most propitious opportunity for tailing. That's why it is preferable to approach on port, so your first tack or jibe will put you on starboard with right of way.

If you want to be aggressive, it's preferable to circle in a clockwise direction. You will then be jibing onto starboard tack and less speed is lost in a jibe, if well executed, than a tack, and better speed coupled with the starboard tack advantage is helpful to achieve tailing.

More often than not, since both skippers are pretty savvy in an America's Cup match, a tailing position is seldom achieved with the first tack or jibe. To gain it eventually, it is essential to achieve better speed in your circling. Avoid too tight turns. My favorite ploy is to sail an oblong circle, reaching for awhile on port tack to build speed before bearing off smartly into a jibe. If the other boat tries to turn inside you, she can't maintain speed and superior speed is very helpful. If you have better speed you can then make a quick jibe or sharp tack, cut inside your adversary, and gain the tailing position. Even if you don't, superior speed will keep you from getting tailed closely and blocked. To maintain speed, main and jib must be eased smoothly as you bear off to jibe and then trimmed furiously after jibing to

In prestart circling, Enterprise *(right) is close to getting on the tail of* Independence *but not close enough to block her from jibing.*

rebuild speed as you sharpen up. It's an exhausting period for the crews and a mind-draining experience for the skipper and tactician. There are so many variables in this circling exercise, depending on how the other boat maneuvers, that you've got to be quick to change your game plan to fit the developing situation. Circles might be reversed, fakes initiated. If you are the trailing boat, it requires a fine sense of distance to tell whether you can swing and clear the leader's stern and thus continue to block her if she fakes a tack and instead bears off to jibe. If you touch you are out. If too far away you can't block her. The boat being tailed may try to build speed to get far enough ahead to be able to maneuver at will. Or she might kill way suddenly to force an overlap and hence be able to alter course without being blocked. In this case the tailed boat could well become the tailer. It's an exciting and deadly serious game with high stakes.

During all this maneuvering the skipper and tactician of both boats must always be thinking of how far they are from the line. If circling is not broken off at precisely the right time, the boat which appeared to have an advantage might lose out. Never should the tailing boat make one too many circles. If she does the other will come out of the circle nearer the line and in a great position to make the boat astern late for the line. You've got to break off when a bit early, but not too early. A book in itself could be written on all the variables that can occur at a match race start, but daring, judgment of time and distance, and the ability to adjust instantly to a fast changing situation, coupled with a complete knowledge of the right of way rules are essential to be a good match race starter.

The best starters develop a killer instinct; not satisfied with just edging the other boat, once they get the upper hand, they use the time before crossing the line to widen the advantage they have gained. One should think ahead also as to which end to cross. Usually it is better to start with a safe leeward since this will force your adversary to tack into the wash of spectator boats after crossing and also because more often than not the wind tends to back on the first leg of the America's Cup course (often hauling later in the day).

A comfort one can gain when about to engage in a match race start is the thought that the other skipper is probably as nervous about it as you are. That helps remove the butterflies and lets you think more clearly. Once the action starts you are too busy to feel nervous and, in fact, it can be great fun. It's certainly fun when you see your boat getting the upper hand.

We've devoted a great deal of space to starts because they are so important and also to give the reader a better understanding of what's going on during that period of apparently aimless circling. But important as the start is, there is so much more to match racing. Even if behind at the start in an even boat, there are still twenty-four miles to go, during which just one slip by the leading boat can turn the tables. All sailors know the axiom that in a match race the lead boat should cover. The trouble is they know it too well, because it simply isn't always true. It often isn't true if you are leading with a slower boat and sometimes isn't even if the two boats are equal in speed. Assume, for example, that the two boats are equal in speed or you are leading in a slower boat and you cross in the safe leeward position. The trailing boat *must* tack. If you tack with her you will be only one-half length ahead. If she is faster that lead is meaningless. If you see a better wind ahead or a favoring slant, or if you feel her tack takes her into unfavorable spectator wash, then *don't* tack to cover. If you are right you can build a really substantial lead. If you do get into a better slant or more wind, she will be forced to tack back and will have lost not only by taking two extra tacks, but also by not getting into the better wind as soon as you. Never in the race will you have such a golden opportunity to build a half length lead into a lead of five lengths *or sometimes a lot more.* And a five to ten length lead, even in a slower boat, is hard to overcome. Hence, *early in the race,* unless your boat is much faster, if you start with a slight lead and *you like where you are going, don't tack immediately to cover.* After all, if you're sailing for the America's Cup, you and your tactician can't be too stupid, and if you feel you're going the right way, the odds are greatly in your favor that you are. So trust your own judgment and don't cover until you've built a good lead. If it backfires and you lose the lead, the press will say how dumb you were, but it will seldom backfire. If, on the other hand, you like where the other boat is going after she tacks, you must go with her, looking for a later opportunity to build a lead. The important thing to remember is that a one length lead is far from safe early in the race and you as leader should look for an opportunity to build it by not covering when the boat astern tacks.

Courageous used this tactic in the first mile of each race against *Australia*

Weatherly *crossing* Gretel *in the second race in 1962. The two boats were this close throughout the race. By careful covering* Weatherly *stayed on top on the windward leg but was passed on the spinnaker reach to the finish.*

in the 1977 match and quickly built large leads. These leads widened very little during the next twenty-three miles, proving that the two boats were more closely matched than most people realized. And also proving the merits of not always covering early in the race.

In the 1970 match, *Intrepid* beat the faster *Gretel* by almost always going where her skipper and tactician thought best, not just early in the race. That's an extreme example of the merits of not covering when ahead, but I don't think *Intrepid* would have won any other way. In chapter ten this fascinating match will be discussed in greater detail.

Courageous *is about to blanket* Independence. *Less than a minute after this photo was taken she swept by.*

If you are ahead try to drive your opponent onto what you consider to be the unfavored tack. It is difficult to blanket the boat behind on both tacks but easy to sit right on her on one tack. Blanket her, therefore, when you feel she is on the preferred tack, thus forcing her onto the unfavored tack. And until you have a good lead, don't be too hasty to tack to cover. By delaying your cover you will increase your lead substantially, if in truth you are going the right way.

If you round the weather mark with a slight lead and the other boat sails high of the rhumb line, you can often build your lead by resisting the

After losing in light air to Columbia, *the crew of* Sceptre *(right) kept saying, "Just wait till we get a hard wind." But when it did blow they were annihilated. This photo was taken right after the start, which* Columbia *also won.*

temptation of going up with her. Unless the wind increases in the latter part of the reach, she will lose as she comes down to the jibe mark.

Another time not to cover when leading is when you find you are losing in a tacking duel. In this instance break off the cover while still ahead and when you feel you are on the preferred tack. If you are right, the trailing boat will have to tack back and follow you, losing by two extra tacks and by being late getting to the favored side of the course. You better be good at determining which is the favored tack, but chances are you will be.

If ahead on a run, position yourself on the leeward bow of the other boat, on the very brink of being blanketed. You can always keep your wind clear by sharpening up and will increase speed as you sharpen up. But if you get dead ahead of the boat astern, when she jibes and you jibe to cover, she could well be right on your wind. That's why the position which seems precarious is actually much the safer. And if when slightly ahead on a run don't hesitate to jibe immediately if you get lifted. It's a golden opportunity to widen your lead, an opportunity which will be lost if you wait for the boat astern to jibe first. If the leader jibes when lifted and the boat astern elects not to jibe, the boat astern is almost certain to drop farther astern.

Don't be misled by all I've been saying about the merit of not always covering when leading in a match race. All of this applies only when you have a slight lead and hope to build it or if you know your boat is slower or, at best, even in speed. Once you have a substantial lead, unless your boat is much slower, it is imperative to cover the boat astern *even when you are quite certain she is going the wrong way.* That is when the axiom "when ahead cover" is absolutely true, simply because you could be wrong. Lowell North in *Enterprise* lost several races to *Courageous* in 1977 by not following this precept. I remember one race in particular (though there were a number of less extreme examples). *Enterprise* was about ten lengths ahead at the end of the run and when she rounded held port tack, heading towards a fine looking breeze to the south. With only one leg to go Turner had no option but to tack to starboard toward what appeared to be much lighter wind to the east. For awhile *Enterprise* gained, doubling her lead. Then the breeze to the south died and at the same time built in the east. *Courageous* got the new wind first and won by a distance of a full mile. Yes, I thought it looked better to the south. I'm sure Turner thought so too. But North was dead wrong in not covering and staying between his opponent and the mark when he had a big lead late in the race and had good boat speed. He picked the only possible way to lose. It matters not a whit how far you are ahead at the finish, just so long as you are ahead. Covering and taking extra tacks to ensure staying between your opponent and the mark is apt to reduce your lead, but when the lead is substantial or when nearing the finish, it *must be done even when you feel a different tack is better.*

It is wise with a big lead to make somewhat of a loose cover to reduce the number of tacks and the possibility of an override, a torn sail, or other breakdown. But with a big lead this must never be done to such an extreme that you don't stay pretty much between the other boat and the mark.

What if you are behind in a match race? There it's smart to try a tacking duel, and if you see you are either holding your own or gaining, keep it up. Especially late in the race, keep tacking even if you aren't gaining because the more tacks you force on the boat ahead, the greater the chance she will suffer a breakdown which will let you through.

But early in the race, if you aren't gaining in a tacking duel, knock it off and try to get clear air on what you consider to be the favored tack. With the race still young it is vital to stay close, waiting for an opportunity to break through later rather than taking a flyer. Be particularly suspicious if the boat ahead lets you go off by yourself. She must be sure her tack is better, and unless you have a firm sound reason to believe yours is better, follow the boat ahead. In a twenty-four-mile race there will be many opportunities to close ground. *So stay close.* This is particularly true if you have a faster boat. Remember that wishful thinking wins very few boat races. If *Gretel II* had followed this tactic of staying close and following *Intrepid* rather than blindly splitting when behind, I feel she would have won the 1970 match and the America's Cup. The only time to try to split or to continue a tacking duel which you are losing is late in the race when there is no other possible way to break through.

And when behind, avoid being driven to the lay line, thus allowing the leading boat to blanket you on a long last tack to the mark.

The boat astern can almost always gain by tacking in headers or jibing on lifts. The leader is apt to be thinking more about covering than he is about widening his lead, and this gives you a chance to close the gap and be in a position to gain the lead if you get a break or if you're opponent goofs.

Initiating a jibing duel is also a sound tactic for the trailing boat on a run.

Basic match racing tactics call for Intrepid *to tack on* Gretel II *in this situation. In the 1970 match, however, they did only when they felt* Gretel *was on the favored tack.*

Not only is she apt to blanket the leader at least momentarily as she crosses her stern, but there is also the possibility that the leader will make a poor jibe while you keep your chute full. It's easier for the boat astern to make a good jibe because the crew is forewarned as to the time of the jibe. Unless she gets headed as the boat astern jibes, the leader must jibe immediately after she sees the tailing boat bearing off to jibe, and hence she has a bit less time to get ready. America's Cup crews are so good that this isn't a great problem, but still it is a slight advantage for the boat astern to know in advance when she will jibe.

Once the jibe has been completed it is essential to head well high of course to rebuild the boat speed lost while jibing. This is particularly true in light air. Apparent wind must then be brought *forward of the beam,* even on a running leg, bearing off only after speed has been rebuilt. This is particularly true for the leading boat in order to keep her wind clear, but it applies also to the boat astern unless it is blowing so hard that little speed is lost while jibing and a high course isn't required to regain speed.

Match racing should be approached like a game of chess, thinking always about how you might thwart your opponent. It is a special and utterly fascinating type of sailing. To be good at it you've got to keep cool, be analytical, and avoid wishful thinking or flyers in hopes of catching the boat ahead of you. If you're ahead, don't be suckered into doing something foolish. One example of foolishness or wishful thinking on the part of a boat astern is a fake tack. It will *never* work in America's Cup competition because the tactician on the leading boat will be watching all through the tack and will see you abort yours. All that will happen is that you will drop farther astern.

There are so many variables to match racing that this single chapter can't begin to cover all of them. I hope only that it has given the reader a little better insight as to what goes on out there. And for those who partake in match racing and in the America's Cup itself, one parting shot of advice. Have fun doing it. I can guarantee you will sail better if you do!

Weetamoe *(left) and* Enterprise *in prestart maneuvering in the final 1930 trial. Compare* Weetamoe's *much larger wooden spreaders and her wooden spar with the trim metal over on* Enterprise.

Chapter IV
Why the Early Leader Often Loses

No bigger error can be made than to assume that the American boat with the best record in the June and/or July trials will surely become the eventual defender. There have been too many instances when the early leader has fallen flat in the final selection trials in August. Sometimes it has been close in the early races between two or more contenders: *Columbia, Vim,* and *Weatherly* in 1958; *Weatherly* and *Nefertiti* in 1962; *Intrepid* and *Valiant* in 1970; and *Courageous* and *Intrepid* in 1974. Eventually the first named in each instance came through in August.

Only twice in the past fifty years has the early leader dominated all three sets of trials: *Ranger* in 1937 and *Intrepid* thirty years later. In 1977 *Courageous* did well in June, faltered a bit in July, but then came on strong in the final trials of August.

But in three other years the early leader failed dramatically when selection was on the line. In 1930 *Weetamoe* won the majority of the early races but *Enterprise* overtook her at the end. In 1934 *Yankee* appeared to have a lock on selection but then *Rainbow* nosed her out, winning the climactic race by a scant one second! An equally big turnaround (I am happy to say) came in 1964. *American Eagle* won the first fourteen races, being undefeated in both the June and July trials. At that stage *Constellation* had a rather dismal seven win, eight loss score. In the New York Yacht Club cruise, *Constellation* began turning things around by winning four and losing two while *American Eagle* was winning two and losing four. In the final trials *Constellation* won nine races and lost but one, while *Eagle* won four and lost six, all six losses being to *Constellation*. *American Eagle* never lost a race except to *Constellation* all year long but despite her sensational early showing, when the summer was over *Eagle*'s record in races sailed against *Constellation* was eight wins and ten losses and in the final trials, one win and six losses.

How were these dramatic turnarounds possible, and how, even when there is no big turnaround, does it happen so often that the eventual winner doesn't take charge until the final trials in August? There were different reasons for the three most dramatic comebacks, reasons we will delve into soon. But certain basic aspects in every campaign make the early races somewhat unindicative of what is to come. The June trials are not unlike spring training games in baseball or exhibition games in other sports. It is a time to experiment, to learn, and to test—a time when you would like to win but also a time when you don't feel you have to. The June trials are called "preliminary trials," and contenders are told by the selection committee that the results count very little in making the eventual choice. The July trials are called "observation trials," and as the name implies, the selection committee is watching with more care and making at least initial judgements. The trials in August are the "selection trials," the ones you *must* win to be selected to defend the America's Cup.

The June trials are frequently used for testing new sails. In 1974 on *Courageous* we persisted with a Kevlar mainsail all through June. It was a real dog to start with, and even after lots of recutting, it remained a dog. We stuck with it, though, hoping it could be recut into a breakthrough sail and knowing that a poor record in June would not hurt our chances. It did, however, hurt my confidence, even though I knew the main was poor. It hurt in another way because it was not until August that we had our final sail inventory, and even in August we were not sure which sails were best for each condition. Too much experimenting early can be harmful because the summer passes all too rapidly and everything must be sorted out prior to August.

On some boats the early races are used to help in crew selection. Each boat has several alternate crew members and in some cases these are given a chance in June to prove their ability. The boats which do not rotate, but instead use the "first team" in June are apt to be handled more smoothly in the early going.

But none of the above can explain fully the dramatic come-from-behind victories of *Enterprise* in 1930, *Rainbow* in 1934, or *Constellation* in 1964.

In 1930 many magazine covers pictured *Weetamoe* as the likely defender. Although *Enterprise* was generally sailed better throughout the summer, she simply did not match *Weetamoe*'s speed. Drastic action had to be taken and it came in the form of replacing her spruce mast with an aluminum one. The mast was first used on 3 June and at once she seemed like a different (and far better) boat. The designer, Starling Burgess, however, wanted to make some rigging changes and hence the lighter of her two wooden spars was restepped. This may have lulled *Weetamoe* (which also had an aluminum spar in reserve) into believing that *Enterprise*'s metal spar was a flop. In any event, they stuck with their wooden one on the basis that it would be foolish to change a winning combination.

When *Enterprise* restepped her metal spar for the observation trials, she encountered more rigging problems, but by the time the final trials began all the bugs had been ironed out. The new spar weighed only 4,000 pounds, 600 pounds less than the lighter of her two spruce spars. The wood spreaders were replaced by steel ones for an additional saving of 384 pounds aloft. The importance of this weight saving is dramatized by the fact that the center of gravity of her rig was 65 feet above the metacenter (which is 3 feet above the waterline). The lead keel was 14.5 feet below the metacenter, a ratio of 4.5 to 1. Hence for every pound saved aloft they could dispense with 4.5 pounds of ballast without affecting stability. Or if the ballast remained constant, stability and hence heavy weather performance would be improved. There is also much less tendency to hobbyhorse with a light rig.

Not only was the aluminum spar lighter, it also was a more efficient shape and dimension. The aluminum mast was 18 inches in diameter at deck, tapering to 8 inches aloft. The wooden was of elliptical shape 27 inches by 20 inches at deck, tapering to a circular shape of 9¾ inches diameter at the head.

While the new mast was the dominant change and biggest reason for improvement, other important modifications were made to *Enterprise* prior to the final trials. Her original boom was replaced by a Park Avenue boom, so named because its upper surface was four feet wide one-third of the way back from the mast. Two men could walk down it abreast. It weighed 2,330 pounds, 365 pounds more than the original rectangular boom, but it permitted a more efficient sail shape. Transverse tracks allowed the main to assume an efficient camber, and by adjusting the stops on the slides, the camber could be modified to suit the wind conditions—more curve for light air, less for heavy air.

The main was recut to fit the new boom. A smaller rudder was installed, reducing wetted surface by one percent. They also installed a new jib topsail winch. And to demonstrate Mike Vanderbilt's thoroughness, the compass was reswung to ensure the new boom had not affected its accuracy (it had not). When the final trials began *Enterprise* was as ready as a boat could be and ready with a lot of new tricks up her sleeve.

The most vital races were against *Weetamoe,* and *Enterprise* with her new lease on life won both of them, the first over a light leeward-windward course, the second in a twenty-five knot nor'easter. The latter was the one where the new mast brought her into her own, but few people know how close she came to losing the spar in that one. A fitting designed to keep her spreaders locked in position failed, and the afterguard was horrified to see them swinging badly out of line. They debated dropping out until Starling Burgess thought of hooking ends of the spinnaker halyard to the spreaders to keep them in line. It worked!

In writing about the incident in his book *Enterprise,* Mike said: "Every country, every individual, every boat has a high spot, a point of climax in his or its history, which often spells the difference between success or failure. I consider this the high spot of *Enterprise's* career. Had Starling Burgess failed to find the right answer, had we either withdrawn or lost our mast, I do not believe we would ever have defended the Cup. Little things often determine momentous questions."

The selection committee attempted more races, but the weather failed to cooperate. On two successive days there was virtually no wind. On the third day, 27 August, there was enough to start, with *Weetamoe* paired with *Whirlwind* and *Enterprise* with *Yankee.* This one was called when there was no chance of finishing within the time limit.

That night the announcement was made that *Enterprise* had been selected to defend the America's Cup. When the chips were down she had made the key moves to be able to defeat her main rival. Although they met in just two races in the final trials, one was in light air, the other in heavy, and she was impressive in both. An editorial in *Yachting* concluded with the words "No unbiased person will cavil at the ultimate selection."

Four years later Mike Vanderbilt had an even tougher uphill battle sailing *Rainbow* against *Yankee. Yankee* was improved in the four years since her launching and proceeded to beat the new boat in the first ten races they had against each other. The margins varied from twelve seconds to more than fifteen minutes but from 24 June through 15 August it was always *Yankee* first, *Rainbow* second. To make matters worse *Rainbow* lost both in light air and heavy.

Weetamoe had also been modified, but for the worse and never was in contention even with the seemingly outclassed *Rainbow.*

Prior to the Astor Cup Race on 16 August with the final trials just a week away, Vanderbilt decided something drastic had to be done. What he did was add a full five tons of ballast to *Rainbow.* Whether or not the additional ballast was the sole reason, the improvement was electrifying. *Rainbow* beat her arch rival by six minutes thirty-nine seconds and the next day won the King's Cup by three minutes twenty-two seconds.

She still entered the final trials on 22 August with a two win ten loss record against *Yankee,* but momentum was on her side and *Rainbow's* afterguard thought that despite the lopsided score their chances were roughly even.

The euphoria did not last long. After beating *Weetamoe* by a sound margin in the first race, *Rainbow* met *Yankee* on 23 August and got clobbered by more than six minutes. A note in Rainbow's log read "5:09 *Yankee* finishes. Good night. 5:15 we finished, licked by 6'20". This will come near finishing our hash." The only encouraging aspect was the fact that *Rainbow* lost partly by setting a quadrilateral jib instead of the genoa *Yankee* had used. This was a mistake they would not repeat. Still *Yankee* had now improved her record to eleven to two, and time was running out.

The next two days *Yankee* and *Rainbow* took turns beating *Weetamoe* which was then excused from further competition. On 27 August the *final* final races began. *Rainbow* rebounded to beat *Yankee* by more than three minutes in winds between six and nine miles per hour.

The next day in a thirteen mile breeze *Rainbow* led narrowly at the first mark, and then *Yankee* broke a strut on her mast and had to retire. Although the committee then canceled the race, *Yankee*'s breakdown was a black mark. A blacker mark was administered on the next race day, 30 August. In winds ranging from sixteen miles per hour at the start to fourteen at the finish *Rainbow* led at every mark to win by over two minutes.

What proved to be the clincher occurred the next day over a thirty mile windward-leeward race, starting in ten knots, finishing in fourteen. *Rainbow* led at the weather mark by one minute twenty-eight seconds. On the run home with Frank Paine calling the spinnaker trim, *Yankee* kept closing. At the finish the two yachts were bow to bow. When the gun went no one on either vessel or on the spectator boats knew who won. Only the man on the line did. The official time difference was one second but it was less than that. *Rainbow* was three feet ahead!

By that slim margin she was selected to defend the America's Cup, and to defend it masterfully against the faster *Endeavour*.

While *Enterprise* and *Rainbow* came with a rush at the end by making changes to the boat, *Constellation*'s come-from-behind victory over *American Eagle* was achieved by making personnel changes. It is awkward for me to have to credit myself for much of the turnaround, but the fact is that when Eric Ridder was steering he never beat *American Eagle* and after I became helmsman we beat her in all but one trial race (losing two other fleet races on the New York Yacht Club cruise, in one of which we lost our mast). The other key crew change was getting Rod Stephens aboard as tactician and crew boss. He made the whole operation gel.

The only reason crew changes could make a difference was the fact that *Constellation* and *American Eagle* were quite evenly matched. *Eagle* won the first fourteen races because Bill Cox was sailing her superlatively well. I am convinced, however, that *Constellation* was slightly faster, certainly to windward and on a run. *Eagle* maybe had a slight edge on a reach. With *Connie* (as we often referred to her) being faster upwind, all we needed was to be close at the start with clear air. I found her an easy boat to feel, and by settling her into her groove and letting her do her stuff, we were usually in command of the race within two miles. Thereafter it was a matter of avoiding mistakes. It is pretty easy to seem smart if your boat is faster, even a slight bit faster.

I feel that *Constellation*'s late surge was due also to perfection of our sails. We did not have a large inventory (much smaller than *American Eagle*'s) but Ted Hood kept recutting the few we did have until they were perfect. *American Eagle* also had Hood sails and they were good, but whereas we never told Ted what to do on recutting and left everything up to his judgment, Bill Cox kept urging certain modifications.

During the final trials when *Constellation*'s main looked like a fine piece of sculpture, I asked Ted if *Eagle* had one as good. "They used to" was his terse reply. Cox is a lot more scientific than I am, but whoever told a skilled surgeon how to operate? Bill Cox just might—one of his few weaknesses.

There is one other factor, perhaps the most important one of all, which works to the advantage of a boat which is behind in the early going. I refer to the pressure which builds on the early leader. If you are winning big like *Ranger* did in 1937 or *Intrepid* in 1967 one's confidence grows and all the pressure is on the tailenders who know that only a miracle can save them. But if you are winning by small margins just the reverse is true. This is particularly true if you feel the boat you are beating is as fast or faster than yours. You keep wondering if you can keep on edging them and you worry because you know that all the wins you are racking up won't mean a damn if you do not win in the final trials.

I know that Bill Cox was running scared all through his winning streak of fourteen straight. His crew thought they had it made but Bill was too smart for that. He knew *Constellation* had latent speed and he worried about the time we would get it out of her. Bill kept sailing well, but I sensed that he did his most masterful sailing in the early races. Once we started to win, he did not sail quite as well as he had earlier.

Much the same happened to me ten years later. *Courageous* was the early favorite and in the early going I think I sailed well. But when we failed to live up to our favorite's role and had only an even record against *Intrepid,* I started to press, thought less clearly, and did not sail as well. Those sailing the underdog boat or the early loser which shows good speed can keep loose because they know that matters cannot get worse and might very well get better. It is the same as being close behind in an individual race and gaining. All your thoughts are on gaining the lead while the leader's thoughts are on how to maintain it. There is much more pressure on the leader. The trailing boat calls the moves, thinks positively, and feels there is a real chance to get past while the leader cannot help but worry about losing the lead. His tacks are apt to be hurried and in general it is harder to keep a cool head.

An America's Cup summer is a long one and the stakes are so high that it is almost impossible to stay relaxed. And relaxed sailors who are having fun are sure to sail to their best ability. Believe me, it is easier to stay relaxed when you are losing because any change has to be for the better. The only time I felt any pressure once I started sailing *Constellation* was after we had won a number of races but still had not been selected. I began to wonder if we could keep on beating that formidable opponent, Bill Cox. Finally we lost a final trial race on a flukey day. We lost only because of a drastic wind shift which I had called wrong, and I realized that we were not apt to do that again. The next day, with our winning streak broken, we went out full of confidence, led throughout, and gave *Eagle* one of the worst trouncings of the entire summer. That night we were selected as defender.

Chapter V
The Role of Computers

Maybe it's my unscientific mind. Maybe it's because I'm an instinctive, seat of the pants sailor. Maybe it's because I feel that in 1974 overattention to the role of a computer helped do me in. Maybe it is for some other reason. But let me say loud and clear that the supposed benefit from computers is grossly exaggerated, especially in America's Cup competition.

Don't get me wrong. They are wonderfully efficient and I take my hat off to smart people like Rich McCurdy who have developed them to help sailors get the most out of their boats. They *do* give a reading on when a boat is making her best speed made good to windward. They *do* tell you whether a fast tack or a slow tack gets you closer to the weather mark. They *do,* in the absence of a trial horse, give you a reading on how fast your boat is. They *are* a superlative navigational tool in helping you find the weather mark if a thick fog sets in. They *are* superb in telling you the precise apparent wind angle to expect on the next leg and hence a guide to chute selection. They *are* great in determining the most efficient apparent wind angle and hence course to sail on a running leg to get to the leeward mark faster. In short, as developed by Rich, they do everything they are supposed to do. Yet in America's Cup competition they are not worth a damn!

If you cannot figure all of those things out either instinctively or with the assistance of a simple polar plot, dead reckoning navigation, or a pocket calculator, you should not be sailing for the America's Cup. The trouble with computers in connection with top-level sailing is that they are never wrong in a technical sense but, smart as they are, *they do not think,* do not forecast anything beyond the input that thinking people put into them. And because of their technical virtuosity and efficiency they are apt also to become a crutch and inhibit thinking. The batteries used to power them are heavy and their weight cannot be placed in an optimum position. Moreover, they need constant care to keep them running, and the time thus spent can be better utilized.

Despite their navigational ability, in the one trial race of 1977 sailed in heavy fog no boats found the weather mark and the race was canceled. Whenever fog becomes so thick that you cannot find the mark by dead reckoning the race is apt to be canceled and hence that supposed advantage of a computer is negated. And commencing in 1980 Loran will be allowed which will make it easy to find a mark even in thick fog. On a distance race where no boats are nearby or where boats are of different rating, a computer could be of great benefit in determining whether a helmsman was sailing the best possible speed to windward. But in America's Cup competition you have got a far more efficient measuring device—the boat you are trying to beat. By taking constant bearings and distances on your adversary, you learn immediately whether or not you are gaining or losing—and focusing on the adversary is what match racing is all about.

As for tacking, the position of the other boat and the speed of her tack should govern whether you tack fast or slow. If a fast tack will allow you to sit on her wind, then that is the sort of tack to take, not the slower one which a computer says is better. Moreover, you do not need a mechanical device to prove the most efficient speed of tack when not in a position to blanket the other boat. You learn it pretty fast. In 1974 *Courageous* was

Partly hidden by Halsey Herreshoff is the ingenious computer **Courageous** *used in 1974, though not always to her benefit.*

beating *Intrepid* in the tacking duels of the June trials. Then I thought constantly of the position of the other boat in determining the optimum speed of tack. Between the June and July trials we practiced tacking for hours using the computer to determine the most efficient tacking speed. And in July we lost most of the tacking duels against *Intrepid!*

Computers are most efficient in determining the best sailing angle on a run. But this is easy to calculate almost as accurately by a pocket calculator, by a polar plot, or by simple observation of how you are doing against the other boat. *The other boat*—that is the thing to think about relative to your own. If she is sailing too broad for best speed downwind and you are ahead, it is tactically sound to sail a bit too broad yourself to better cover, just so long as you are gaining or holding even with a comfortable lead. Sailing higher and increasing your lead thereby will not work for long because your opponents will soon spot it and emulate you. Moreover, if they tend to sail too broad, why educate them? There may come a time when they are ahead, and if they sail too broad an angle, you will be able to close the gap before they catch on to why you are gaining.

As for predicting the apparent wind angle on an ensuing leg, computers are precisely accurate. And this, coupled with knowledge of what spinnaker is best for a given angle and weight of wind, should make them useful in this role. But their mere virtuosity in this respect can also do you in if you become overdependent on it and stop thinking of the tactical situation. This is precisely what happened in a 1974 final trial race against *Intrepid* where we lost a lead. We had a five-length lead at the weather mark and were preparing to set our three-quarter ounce tri-radial reaching chute for the ensuing leg. A check against the computer, however, told us that the half-ounce floater would be a shade faster since the wind had lightened and hauled a bit, making the reach slightly broader than usual. Since the computer was always right in such calculations, we stopped thinking and set it. The first stadimeter reading confirmed the computer's accuracy since we gained five yards against *Intrepid* which was flying a three-quarter ounce radial. Then she started to gain. We lulled ourselves into believing she just had a puff, and by the time we woke up to what had happened she was nearly abeam. We switched to our three-quarter ounce spinnaker, but it was too late and she was by us.

Here is what happened. The wind came slightly ahead and increased almost imperceptibly and all of a sudden the floater was ineffective. Worst of all, it is suicide to try to luff with a floater, and hence to the surprise of unknowing spectators we held our course and must have appeared to have no fight in us. If we had not had such a blind faith in the computer, we would have thought ahead and realized that a slight header would ruin its effectiveness and also make us unable to defend ourselves. We would have deduced also that the probability was that *Intrepid* would not set a floater and in match racing it is basic that when ahead you match the opponent's weapons.

But what if we had set a three-quarter ounce chute and *Intrepid* a floater and the wind had remained constant, making the floater more effective? No big deal—we might have lost a length but certainly not our entire lead. All we would have had to do was sail a few degrees high to make the three-quarter ounce chute effective during the minute or two it took us to get the floater ready. If *Intrepid* followed us she would lose ground with her floater. If she sailed her own course she would be a length or two closer but on our leeward quarter—not a favorable position from which to pass on a reaching leg. That is the way sound sailors think and computers cannot reason like the human brain.

I asked Ted Turner a year ago what he thought of computers for America's Cup sailing. Without a moment's hesitation he replied, "Worthless." Lowell North is more sold on them, but remember who won in 1977. Lowell was probably the best fleet racer of the three at Newport in 1977. But the America's Cup is a match race and mastery of match race tactics is what is needed to come home first, not second. Do not count on a computer to do it for you.

Chapter VI
Why Twelve Meters?

For a number of years after World War II it appeared that the 1937 match between *Ranger* and *Endeavour II* would be the last one sailed for the America's Cup. Rising taxes and the enormous cost of building and campaigning a J-boat made them as extinct as a dinosaur. No challenges were forthcoming.

While no one knows for sure just what it would cost today to design, build, and campaign a J-boat for one year, a conservative estimate is five million dollars, and it could well cost a great deal more. When one realizes that once a J-boat is no longer a winner, her resale value is nil (many were scrapped within a year or two of their building) it is no wonder that no one was interested. To complicate matters further the deed of the gift did not allow competition in smaller boats.

But there were feelers from abroad about the possibility of reviving the competition in smaller boats and, thus encouraged, the New York Yacht

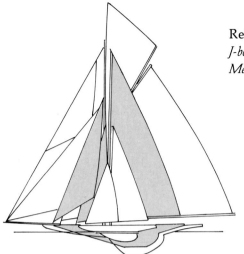

Reliance *was the largest defender, dwarfing the* J-boats *(shaded drawing). Both make the Twelve Meter, drawn to the same scale, look tiny.*

Club looked into the possibility of getting the deed altered. Commodore Henry Sears and past Commodore Harry Morgan were able to convince the courts that the deed should be changed, and it is only because of their efforts that the America's Cup races are alive and well.

Once the decision was made to go to smaller boats, it next had to be decided how small and of what type. There were those who felt it should be in boats as small as six meters to open the competition to a broader number. This was shot down on the basis that even though the competition would be keen it simply would not induce the same excitement. If nothing else, America's Cup boats have always been majestic and that fact contributes to the interest that not only yachtsmen but the general public has taken in the event.

A few people felt it should be sailed in a new one-design class but that is an aspect of the deed which I am sure will never be changed. The competition is intended to test not only the sailing ability of the challenger and defender but also the design capability and the technological savvy of the countries involved. This, incidentally, has had the beneficial effect of improving hardware, sails, and seagoing gadgets which then later have applications in the size and the type of boats more of us race.

A more responsible case can be made for sailing the America's Cup in ocean racing type yachts which could be converted to race and cruise after the match. Many people still feel this would make sense. I do not, for a number of basic reasons. The first is the fact that such a boat, if of comparable size to a Twelve Meter, would cost just as much to build. Yet the cost of a Cup boat itself is only about one-third the total cost of a year's campaign. True, such a boat would have a better resale value but when one considers the cost of conversion probably only $100,000 more than a Twelve. While that is still a lot of money, it is only about seven percent of the cost of a campaign.

Another flaw with using ocean racers is the fact that there already exist major events for that type boat—the Fastnet Race, Bermuda Race, the Transpac, the Admiral's Cup, etc. The America's Cup races might then become just another event.

An equally great problem would be the rating rule. Whether one picked the IOR, MHS, or any other rule for ocean racers, it would be far easier to design a boat which would be unbeatable if she happened to experience in the match the very weather she was designed for. This is true to some extent under the International Rule to which Meter boats are designed but to a far lesser degree. It would be a pity if the America's Cup was won or lost by an extreme boat which in effect lucked into it and this danger is minimized under the International Rule.

These lines of reasoning focused attention on Twelve Meters. In my view they are the ideal choice. The fact that they are out-and-out racing boats makes them logical for a closed course match race series. The fact that they are closer winded than other boats gives them appeal. The fact that they slice through a leftover slop or power to windward through a raging sea almost as if (except for the spray) it were not there makes them unique. The fact that in light air they will sail faster than the wind, despite their heavy displacement, gives them a feel which no other boat I have ever sailed can quite equal. Sure, a catamaran is much faster, faster even than a J-boat, but it is entirely different, a toy, albeit an impressive one, as compared to a majestic, powerful machine.

The mere impracticability of a Twelve gives it an allure and excitement. It is the type of boat any sailor would love to sail or to own if he lets his

Models of all defenders and challengers for the America's Cup are on display in the New York Yacht Club. In the foreground is Intrepid *as of 1970, with* Gretel II *behind her. Behind* Gretel II *is* Intrepid *as she was in 1967, with far more lateral plane.*

heart rule his head. And in America's Cup racing, despite all the cerebral shenanigans which go into it, emotion remains a vital part. Twelves are emotional boats. They are large enough to be majestic in today's yachting scene, and hence capture the public's fancy. Combine that with the practical aspect of a rule which provides for close competition in a variety of wind ranges and they emerge as an ideal choice. You may question that statement about close competition, but my guess is that the margin between two one-designs would be as great after twenty-four miles of racing as it has been in recent matches between the Twelves. Against *Intrepid* in the 1974 trials we won one race by two seconds, lost another by eleven.

But in final analysis the Twelves are a better choice than an ocean racer primarily because they are exciting thoroughbreds. I am all for ocean racers, would far prefer to own one even if the cost of a Twelve were not out of my reach, but if you were either a jockey or a track nut, which would you rather have in the Kentucky Derby, a field of Percherons or those otherwise impractical animals—thoroughbred race horses?

Chapter VII
The Designers

No one has had a greater impact on the America's Cup than the small group of men who have designed the challengers and defenders. And great credit must go to the American designers for keeping the Cup in this country. George Steeres, designer of *America* one hundred and thirty years ago, started our winning ways by giving her crew a superior boat. With few exceptions the Americans have been blessed with a "better mousetrap" in the matches. Superior sailing has helped us win the Cup but no more so than superior design.

Two American designers stand head and shoulders above all the rest in their influence on the Cup races—Nathaniel G. Herreshoff and Olin Stephens. They are joined by two foreign designers who created the fastest boats in three matches, only to lose out to superior sailing by the American skippers and crews. I refer to Charles Nicholson of England and Alan Payne of Australia.

Nathaniel G. Herreshoff

I've elected to talk only about the years since 1930 but an exception must be made in the case of Herreshoff. Although I never knew him, I feel as though we are old friends. My first boat was a Herreshoff 12½ Bullseye sloop. My dad won the 1924 Bermuda Race in the converted N.Y. 40 *Memory* which Herreshoff designed. He also owned a Fishers Island 31 which excelled on the 1946 New York Yacht Club Cruise, despite being designed about 30 years before most of her competitors. And immediately after World War II I owned and raced a Herreshoff S-boat. All were lovely boats.

Nat's grandson Halsey Herreshoff crewed for me as navigator on *Courageous* in 1974 and was her navigator in the successful defense of the Cup. Nat Herreshoff, therefore, is close to me in many ways and it would be unthinkable even if he were not to exclude him from the list of America's Cup boat designers on the shallow premise that his era preceded the one covered by this book.

Nathaniel Herreshoff was born in 1848 and died ninety years later. For most of his life he lived and worked in Bristol, Rhode Island, from which stemmed his appellation "The Wizard of Bristol." So great was his dominance in the field of designing and building of yachts that, as Bill Robinson points out in his book *The Great American Yacht Designers,* the period of 1890 to 1920 was known as "The Herreshoff Era."

He had equal success in designing both small boats and large, both power and sail. In power boats his 94-foot *Stilleto* set the unofficial but generally accepted speed record. Nat designed her engines too. With a beam of only 11'6" she could cruise effortlessly at 20 knots and in 1895 made an eight hour run at an average speed of 26½ knots. Herreshoff experimented also with sailing catamarans, the first of which was the 25-foot *Amarylis.* He took great delight in reaching past the Fall River steamers, delight too in showing her heels to all the monohulls. He abandoned the type only when they were banned from open competition. It was seventy-five years before catamarans reemerged to any prominence, now being recognized as the fastest of all sailing types.

Nat Herreshoff, the "Wizard of Bristol" whose designs defended the America's Cup in five different matches. No designer has ever so dominated his profession.

Those who might consider fin keels and separate spade rudders as modern would be surprised to see models dating from 1890 in the model room of the New York Yacht Club, designed, of course, by Nat Herreshoff.

One of his most famous yachts was the 71½-foot *Gloriana,* built in 1891. Unlike other boats of the day which featured a deep sharp forefoot and short overhangs, *Gloriana* has a cutaway forefoot below the waterline and long ends protruding both fore and aft from her waterline of 45'4". Long diagonals enabled these ends to increase sailing length when heeled, length which was not then taxed under the rule. She bears more than a casual resemblance to the Twelve Meters of 1958 and 1962. In her initial year she was absolutely unbeatable.

We have just touched on the many famous yachts he designed, but his greatest fame came from designing the six successful America's Cup defenders between 1893 and 1920: *Vigilant, Defender, Columbia* (twice), *Reliance,* and *Resolute.*

Reliance was not only the biggest of the lot but best showed Nat's inventiveness. On a waterline length of 90 feet she was 149 feet overall and 201½ feet from the tip of her bowsprit to the end of her main boom. Her sail area of 16,000 square feet was more than twice that of the J-boat *Ranger* and nearly eight times that of a Twelve Meter. On a reach she was surely the fastest Cup defender of all time, though *Ranger* would have probably beaten her around the course, largely because of her marconi rig which was more efficient to windward.

Reliance was a skimming dish with a very shallow hull to which was affixed an enormously deep keel. It is a wonder such a hull, light as it was, could hold up to the pounding she was subjected to when beating to windward in a hard thrash. But Herreshoff was as practical as he was inventive and devised ways such as laminated frames, and a number of small frames as opposed to the general custom of fewer, more massive ones. Most of her fittings were designed by Captain Nat himself. Nine of her winches, which he also designed, were below deck, including, as Bill Robinson points out in his book, two speed self-releasing ones for wire sheets and backstays. They also had worm gears, multiple speed clutches, and ball bearings, features previously unknown on yachts. These winches were so efficient that some were used on *Ranger* in 1937.

Herreshoff was a unique combination of artist and engineer. *Reliance* was designed from a model as opposed to the present practice of lofting a set of lines. It took him but two days from the very first model to develop her lines in this fashion. The term "an eye for a boat" applied to Nat Herreshoff better than anyone before or since. Only Bob Derecktor of the current top designers still works from models. Could this be one reason why Bob's boats are so sea-kindly as well as fast? Could it also be why when Bob was building *Valiant* for the 1970 Cup campaign he told me before launching that she did not look right to him. *Valiant* turned out to be one of Olin Stephens's few failures.

But Herreshoff was so much more than an artist. Like Derecktor three-quarters of a century later he was a master builder. His Herreshoff Manufacturing Company, which built all his Cup defenders, was the premier yacht yard in the world. Herreshoff got his formal training at M.I.T. and maybe that's why all his inventive, even radical (for the day), ideas worked in practice. He was a master in figuring stresses and a genius in building hulls and fittings which, while lighter than those of competitors, stood up to the work they were asked to do.

The six challengers against *Vigilant, Defender, Columbia, Reliance,* and *Resolute* were up against so much more than good skippers and crews. They were pitted against Nathaniel Herreshoff. No wonder they were trounced!

Olin Stephens

The only other America's Cup defender designer to rival Herreshoff's dominance is Olin Stephens. Olin, with characteristic modesty, would insist that I refer to his firm name of Sparkman & Stephens, but Olin is the resident genius at S&S with a notable assist from his brother Rod when it comes to the design of rigging, fittings, and making things work.

The brothers Stephens got their start with the success of *Dorade,* a breakthrough ocean racer which, though the smallest boat by far in the 1931 transatlantic fleet, finished two days ahead of the next finisher. From there followed such successful ocean racers as *Edlu, Stormy Weather, Baruna, Blitzen, Bolero, Gesture, Finisterre, Dyna, Bay Bea, Tenacious,* and a host of others. Their boats dominated ocean racing (*Finisterre* winning the famed Bermuda Race three straight times) for over thirty years; more than fifty years after their first design, *Obsession,* which came out in 1978, is one of the truly top offshore contenders.

Their successful one designs include the 13½-foot Blue Jay, and 19-foot Lightning plus a host of stock cruising/racing boats for such firms as Tartan Marine, Hinckley, and Nautor. While best known for designing sailboats, some of the most handsome and efficient power yachts and motor sailors have an S&S origin.

Olin was and is perhaps most at home and most successful with the deep narrow boats fostered by the International Rule of measurement. His six-meter *Goose,* designed in 1938 was a breakthrough for the class and forty years later was still winning an occasional race. His twelve-meter *Vim* designed in 1939 was so far ahead of her time that in 1958 she came close to being selected as defender of the America's Cup, the first year it was sailed for by the Twelves. Of three new boats only *Columbia,* also designed by Olin, was able to beat her out.

Like Herreshoff, Olin Stephens's greatest fame came from his success in designing America's Cup defenders. In 1937 he teamed with Starling Burgess in the design of *Ranger,* the greatest of all J-boats. Olin also sailed on *Ranger* as did his brother Rod. The fact that both are crack sailors was of great help in perfecting their designs. Olin knew by feel, not only by calculation, what made a boat really go. In 1958, as already stated, his *Columbia,* sailed by Briggs Cunningham beat his *Vim* with Bus Mosbacher at the helm. *Weatherly,* designed by Phil Rhodes, and Ray Hunt's *Easterner* were badly beaten.

In 1962 the only new American boat was *Nefertiti* designed by Ted Hood, and a revamped *Weatherly,* sailed superbly by Bus Mosbacher, was the winner.

Olin was back in the winner's circle once again in 1964 with *Constellation* which I had the privilege of sailing. She was clearly the cream of the crop. In 1967 he again designed the winning boat *Intrepid,* as close to a breakthrough design among Twelves as *Vim* had been in her day twenty-nine years earlier.

Olin proved himself to be only human by creating a bit of a turkey in the form of *Valiant* in 1970. *Intrepid,* redesigned by Britton Chance for the 1970 match, beat her out as defender. But his failure with *Valiant* showed one of Olin's greatest attributes—an ability to learn from his mistakes and to benefit thereby. *Valiant* did win the June trials by a narrow margin over

Intrepid. I asked Olin how he felt. "Rotten," he said. "I'm afraid all of this year's boats are too heavy, too extreme in length and displacement. *Valiant* may be the worst of them all." He was perhaps too severe in criticizing *Valiant* which did wind up second but dead right in recognizing the weaknesses of all the American boats in that year.

He came back strong for the next challenge in 1974 by creating that great Twelve *Courageous* and also by redesigning *Intrepid* so effectively that she pushed *Courageous* right up to the final race before losing out.

In 1977 *Courageous* won again, only the third boat to defend twice (*Columbia* at the turn of the century and *Intrepid* in 1967 and 1970 being the others). Second to her, beaten largely because she was not as well sailed, was Olin's newest design, *Enterprise.*

Olin has very nearly matched Herreshoff's record of designing six America's Cup defenders. He has five in his own right (*Columbia* in 1958, *Constellation* in 1964, *Intrepid* in 1967, and *Courageous* in 1974 and 1977). In 1937 he had a major role in the design of *Ranger,* though he told me her basic hull design was one developed by Burgess. In 1970 he couldn't really claim credit for *Intrepid* (nor would he want to) because Britton Chance had reworked her design so much that she was in effect a Chance design. In 1980 Olin has a fine chance to tie Herreshoff in having designed six defenders. *Courageous* and *Enterprise* will both be back, joined by *Freedom,* Olin's latest Twelve Meter design. The only non-S&S design will be $\frac{12}{\text{U.S. }32}$, a new design by David Pedrick, so new in fact that as of this writing she is still not named. Olin would like to tie Herreshoff's record (and, by virtue of sharing *Ranger's* design, actually exceed it). The fact that so many America's Cup syndicates and so many top skippers have opted for an S&S design demonstrate Olin's dominance and brilliance.

While yacht design as practiced by Herreshoff was an art, backed up by an engineer's and builder's practicability, Olin's approach is perhaps more analytical and more scientific, backed up by a thorough knowledge and feel of boats. He was the first, together with Ken Davidson of Stevens Institute, to use a towing tank to check a new design (originating with *Ranger*). A tank does not create a design but if one is a past master at analyzing the input from towing a model (and Olin is!) it can tell you which of several models is apt to be faster.

While Herreshoff's full life was wrapped around designing and building (he often slept at the yard) Olin's interests are varied. He loves classical music and is most knowledgeable about it. I went to the London Symphony with him and between acts was astounded to hear him comment on how good the second violinist was. With anyone else I would have expected him to be showing off, but with Olin I'm sure he could detect said violinist's virtuosity. I have also accompanied Olin on a tour of London's art museums, and while I studied art appreciation in college, I felt like a babe in the woods. He paints for relaxation and this heightens his appreciation of the masters.

While Olin is a crack sailor, he has not raced or campaigned his own boat since 1934. He does still race from time to time with owners of his various designs and is always welcomed aboard. But most weekends are spent with his wife Suzie in a hideaway in Massachusetts and most recently Vermont. On the job he is all business and tireless. I have spent two summers with him in connection with the 1964 campaign on *Constellation* and ten years later on *Courageous.* Olin worked from dawn to after dark on perfecting each boat. He watched each race and each practice sail with intensity and shot many rolls of pictures. His comments and suggestions were most helpful, diplomatically presented, and were always listened to.

When around boats he thinks of nothing else. After the 1964 match as *Constellation* was sailing back to Newport in company with *Sovereign,* my wife Charlotte, was on the bow of our tender along with Olin. Olin was saying hardly a word and kept his eyes glued on *Constellation.* Charlotte broke his reverie by asking Olin if he was mentally designing the next defender. Olin laughed and then admitted that that is exactly what he was thinking of and added something to the effect that he was watching the bow and stern overhangs and their minor contribution to sailing length. *Intrepid's* ends three years later were distinctly different, and good as *Constellation* was, *Intrepid* was a definite improvement.

I've talked first about Herreshoff and Stephens since they were the two most dominant designers of Cup boats. The other great designers of America's Cup defenders and challengers will be considered in chronological order, commencing with 1930.

Starling Burgess designed three defenders: Enterprise *in* 1930, Rainbow *in* 1934 *and that super J-boat* Ranger *in* 1937 *in collaboration with Olin Stephens.*

W. Starling Burgess

W. Starling Burgess was the designer of the three J-boat defenders: *Enterprise* in 1930, *Rainbow* in 1934, and *Ranger* in 1937. Were it not for his spectacular success with *Ranger* it would be all too easy to write him off as a good but uninspired designer. But, as Olin Stephens will verify, *Ranger* was primarily a Burgess design and she well deserved the often overused appellation "super boat." In her brief career she never lost a trial race and was the ultimate refinement of the type.

Burgess grew up in boats and the designing of them. His father Edward was a noted designer, including three Cup defenders: *Puritan* 1885, *Mayflower* 1886, and *Volunteer* 1887.

Like Herreshoff and Stephens, Burgess was a sailor as well as a designer and, as recounted in chapter four, it was his ingenuity which kept *Enterprise*'s rig in when a spreader swung loose in the climactic heavy weather race.

For both *Enterprise* and *Rainbow* it was an uphill battle for selection. *Weetamoe,* designed by Clinton Crane, was basically the fastest boat in 1930.

Burgess's greatest contribution to the success of *Enterprise* was not only in the design of her aluminum spar but also in rigging it to stand properly. These were largely "uncharted waters" because heretofore all masts were of wood or steel, but Burgess did his calculations well.

In 1934 it was *Yankee* which was the apparent cream of the crop, but Burgess worked with Vanderbilt to perfect *Rainbow* for the final trials. Attention to detail is vital to bring a racing boat up to peak form and at this Burgess was a master.

Although he usually figured things most scientifically, he made one goof which, while amusing, did have its serious side. Burgess was of slight build and when he was hoisted aloft one day to check the sheave at *Enterprise*'s masthead, he forgot to calculate the weight of *Enterprise*'s main halyard as opposed to his own. As he was nearing her masthead on a bosun's chair, he started to ascend at an ever increasing speed. Shouts to hoist more slowly were to no avail, and he shot up until coming to a jarring stop at the very top. What had happened was the fact that his own weight was so much less than that of the halyard that the halyard, with no one pulling on it, shot him aloft once he neared the top. This demonstrates the massive gear required by the J's. Burgess might still be up there if he hadn't figured out the problem and pulled himself down by means of the two part halyard.

Burgess' masterpiece was *Ranger,* a personal achievement little less noteworthy because Olin had collaborated with him. *Ranger* was primarily Burgess's baby and a superb monument to a successful if not brilliant career as a yacht designer.

Burgess was in competition not only with noted American naval architects such as Clinton Crane *(Weetamoe),* Frank Paine *(Yankee),* and L. Francis Herreshoff *(Whirlwind)* but was also up against the great British designer Charles Nicholson.

Charles Nicholson

Nicholson was like Nat Herreshoff in being not only a naval architect but also a builder. Camper & Nicholsons was to England what the Herreshoff Manufacturing Company was to America.

Charles Nicholson, designer of the British challenger's Shamrock V *(1930),* Endeavour *(1934) and* Endeavour II *(1937).* Endeavour *should have beaten* Rainbow, *and only* Ranger *could have beaten* Endeavour II.

His 1930 challenger *Shamrock V* was a poor example of what was to come. *Enterprise* won with such ease that it is likely any one of the four American contenders could have defended the Cup successfully. I suspect, however, that the fault lay not with *Shamrock*'s hull but with her rig. Compared to the defender's, *Shamrock*'s rig was heavy and complicated, with crude fittings which increased windage and weight aloft. Bedecked with indifferent sails she was no match for *Enterprise.*

But Nicholson recognized these shortcomings and his *Endeavour* four years later sported a clean and efficient rig which one of her crew, Frank Murdock, helped design. She had the type of "Park Avenue" boom *Enterprise* had and her mast was not only of a small diameter but was also trimly stayed and equipped with clean fittings. Most significant, however, was the superb hull form of *Endeavour.* She was larger than *Rainbow* yet was so graceful as to appear smaller. Painted a lovely color blue which to this day bears her name, she was in my view the most beautiful J-boat of all time.

And how she could go! In light air and heavy, both upwind and down, she was a real flyer. In chapter ten we discuss how *Rainbow* managed to beat her after losing the first two races. But *Endeavour*'s loss was no fault of Nicholson. For the first time in the history of the America's Cup the challenger was faster and as *Yachting* reported at the time: "The only man to make no mistakes was *Endeavour*'s designer, Charles Nicholson."

As great as *Endeavour* was, Nicholson was able to improve on her three years later with *Endeavour II.* But the improvement was minor, while *Ranger,* the adversary in 1937, was a quantum leap forward. Had Nicholson had the benefit of tank testing, like Burgess and Stephens, he might have fared better. *Endeavour II* was no slouch, however, and put up a good fight. She was clearly the second fastest J-boat ever built.

Nicholson's reputation as a great designer was made in *Endeavour,* the boat that everyone knew could have and should have lifted the Cup. His reputation as a gentleman was solidified by the fact at no time did he ever blame anyone for failure to win with *Endeavour.* He didn't have to because the yachting world knew *Endeavour* was the best J-boat in the world in 1934, but a lesser man than Charles Nicholson would still have complained, especially when the prize was so great and so obviously within his grasp.

When the America's Cup shifted to Twelve Meters thirty-one years later there were, with the exception of Olin Stephens, a new generation of designers. We've already talked about Olin's resounding successes with a series of Twelves, but who were his adversaries?

David Boyd

In 1958 and 1964 the designer of the challenger was a Scotchman, David Boyd. His credentials were some quite good Six Meter designs, particularly *Circe,* plus a sprinkling of ocean racers and local one designs. There were British designers such as Arthur Robb of greater renown but Boyd was given the nod.

His *Sceptre* created in 1958 had trouble beating some ancient British Twelves in early brushes but improved with tuning. She was best identified by a round barrel-chested forefoot. When Olin Stephens first viewed her

David Boyd, designer of the British challengers Sceptre *and* Sovereign, *which were annihilated by* Columbia *and* Constellation.

hauled out at Newport, he was heard to remark: "Either David or I are awfully wrong." It soon became apparent that it was not Olin who was wrong.

In the 1958 match *Columbia* won easily in light air. Perhaps to keep their hopes up the British kept saying: "Wait till we get a real breeze." But when the strong wind they had been waiting for did arrive, *Sceptre* lost by an equally wide margin. She simply would not go in any kind of seaway and at Newport, in light air as well as heavy, there is always a sea.

In Boyd's defense it should be noted that *Sceptre* had inferior sails and was hurt especially by her crew's predisposition to flying huge oversized spinnakers which simply do not work off Newport, with the possible exception of running in fresh air. Still *Sceptre* was a sure loser even with the finest sails.

She did have one clever and efficient feature, in the form of a large crew cockpit which allowed both winches and crew weight to be lower. Such a cockpit was subsequently barred but I suspect it was a good idea and that without it *Sceptre* would have been still slower.

Six years later Boyd was commissioned to design the British challenger *Sovereign* on the flimsy pretense that he now had experience with the type. In *Sovereign* he replaced Sceptre's barrel bow with a fine one, designed to better slice through a sea. The trouble was that above the waterline *Sovereign* had a great deal of flare and as a result she lifted to each sea and hobbyhorsed to a disgraceful extent. Again it was the wrong way to cope with a sea. She was hindered also by sails which were no match for *Constellation*'s and by crude and heavy rigging and fittings aloft, reminiscent of the cumbersome gear *Shamrock* was festooned with thirty-four years earlier. It made you wonder if the British would ever learn and was a real step backward from the beautiful and efficient *Endeavour.*

Even though *Sovereign* lost by the greatest margins in America's Cup history, I do not think she was intrinsically as bad as her record and certainly an improvement on *Sceptre.* I base this largely on the fact that I raced *Constellation* against her two years later off of Marseilles. *Sovereign* was then outfitted with Hood sails, and I got the impression that though we beat her in four straight races there was little to choose between the two boats as long as there was not much sea running. This was confirmed when I was persuaded to skipper *Sovereign* for one race after the series was over. True, we got the start, and true, a sea never did build up and this helped me. Still, we gave *Constellation* a real licking. When I later reported our win to David Boyd he was beside himself with relief, accepting the fact that he and *Sovereign* were now vindicated. The truth of the matter was that *Sovereign* was still outclassed whenever the sea built and it always builds at Newport, if not by the wind then from the wash of spectator boats. David Boyd was a charming, diffident and modest man but, based on *Sceptre* and *Sovereign,* far from an inspired designer. I am sure that with equal sails and sailed equally, *Constellation* would beat *Sovereign* even in smooth water and kill her as the seas increased. *Sovereign* can best be characterized as an average Twelve, better than the dog that *Sceptre* was, but no match for the likes of her good contemporaries such as *Constellation, American Eagle, Gretel, Weatherly,* or *Nefertiti.*

Phil Rhodes and Bill Luders

I am lumping Phil Rhodes and Bill Luders together simply because they both deserve credit for *Weatherly,* the successful defender in 1962. Rhodes designed her in 1958, and although well sailed that year by Artie Knapp, she was beaten not only by *Columbia* but also by the aged *Vim.* She was in there in

Phil Rhodes designed only one Twelve Meter but Weatherly *was a close contender in 1958 and was the successful defender in 1962 against* Gretel.

many races, won quite a few of them, particularly in light air and showed a great deal of promise. You have to be just the slightest bit slower to lose in a match race and *Weatherly* was a question of being close but no cigar. Rhodes was a successful designer of a number of fine ocean racers such as *Caribbee, Escapade,* and the Bermuda Race winner, *Kirawan.* He was, however, inexperienced with the International Rule and had never designed a Twelve prior to *Weatherly.* That she came so close, despite being third best is to his credit.

Bus Mosbacher, who beat her with *Vim* in 1958 saw enough in *Weatherly* to accept the role of skipper of her for the 1962 campaign.

For 1962 she remained basically a Rhodes design but Luders was brought in to advise on modification. It will never be completely clear how much Luders did contribute. Her stern was shortened, weight was saved in other ways, and her keel shape was modified. Rhodes was in on these modifica-

tions but so was Luders, and to whom the greatest credit should go for her improvement the world will never know. Rhodes appeared to resent Luders's involvement, and Luders has had little to say about how far his ideas might have differed from those of Rhodes or to whom the greatest credit should go.

But no one will argue that she was improved. The fact that Bus Mosbacher was now at her helm certainly helped. A great skipper always makes a designer seem smart. But in any event, *Weatherly* prevailed not only over the 1958 defender *Columbia* but also over the one new boat, Ted Hood's *Nefertiti*. *Neffie* could beat her in a breeze but *Weatherly* was the cream of the crop in light to moderate and vastly improved in a breeze over her form four years earlier. She had to be improved, had to be well sailed in the match itself to prevail over a design by a new designer of Twelve Meters, Alan Payne of Australia. Phil Rhodes doesn't rank at or near the top of America's Cup designers, but he was a designer of great talent, especially at home with beamy, fast ocean racers. In an era where deep narrow ocean racers were in vogue he developed extremely fast broad centerboarders. He also was the leading motor sailer designer of his era and had a number of outstanding motor yachts to his credit. He hardly ever designed a slow boat and never an ugly one. *Weatherly* was the first International Rule boat he ever designed and to come so close on the first crack shows his ability. He was at a disadvantage in not being an active sailor or racing man, but he knew how to design boats for others to enjoy and do well in.

Bill Luders, on the other hand, was one of the country's outstanding skippers. When the International One Design Class was in its heyday with such luminaries as Cornie Shields, Artie Knapp, Bill Cox, Bus Mosbacher, George Hinman, my dad and myself all competing, Bill Luders was always up there and won as many races as any. Moreover, he did not race as seriously or intensely, having other interests such as tennis at which he was very good. Though a sound designer, I suspect the changes he recommended to *Weatherly* were of the sort a keen sailor would suggest, a sailor who had an instinctive feel of what makes a boat go.

In 1964 he proved his ability as a designer in creating *American Eagle,* the apparent shoo-in for selection until *Constellation*'s late surge.

Alan Payne

Of all the designers of America's Cup challengers only Charles Nicholson and Alan Payne designed boats faster than the defender. Payne really exceeded Nicholson since he designed one boat that was surely faster, *Gretel II* in 1970 and prior to her, *Gretel* which in 1962 was better than *Weatherly* in a breeze and perhaps her equal in light to moderate.

Payne was unfortunate in 1962 in having his boat up against Bus Mosbacher who surely got the very most out of *Weatherly.* He was unfortunate too in that *Gretel*'s owner Frank Packer mucked up the works by changing *Gretel*'s navigator at the last moment and in deciding only at the eleventh hour that Jock Sturrock was to be her skipper. Jock was a fine sailor but, as I know from first hand experience, it is distracting to have an owner looking over your shoulder and second-guessing your every move. Jock sailed well but Bus and his crew sailed better and better sailing decided the issue, although *Gretel* did win one race. *Gretel* was a fine Twelve and in at least one respect was a step ahead of any other. She was the first to have

Alan Payne, designer of Gretel *(1962)* and Gretel II *(1970). The former could have won and the latter should have.*

her coffee-grinder winches cross-connected so that by shifting a clutch those grinding on the windward winch could give power to the leeward one. This permitted four men instead of two to grind in the genoa, a great edge in a heavy weather tacking duel. They put this to good use in the second race of the match, the race which *Gretel* eventually won.

In 1970 *Intrepid,* as revamped by Britton Chance, was faster than *Gretel II* in hard going but everyone but Chance feels she was slower in light air and equal at best in moderate going. In Chapter Ten we describe how *Gretel* managed to lose. It surely was not Alan Payne who was at fault. He had designed but two Twelve Meters but each one in her maiden year was probably the fastest in the world.

In 1974 in *Courageous* we brushed against *Gretel II.* Until *Courageous*'s sails got perfected the two boats were locked in. I am not implying that *Gretel* was as fast as *Courageous* but even when she was four years old she was very, very close.

Alan Payne is not only an extremely competent designer but one of the nicest people you could hope to meet. He loves boats, has an instinctive feel about them to supplement his technical savvy, and loves to talk about them. While not shy in the sense of Herreshoff and Stephens, he is quiet (except when talking about boats), is unassuming and so modest about his own ability that one has to find out for oneself that he is one of the world's finest yacht designers. He has the valuable asset of not feeling he knows it all and, like Olin, is always eager to learn. On top of it all, he is a warm and thoroughly pleasant human being. It is a sad commentary about the profession, at least in Australia, that this superlative designer is unable to pursue yacht design as a sole profession, though he will make time available if an inviting design opportunity presents itself—say, another challenger for the America's Cup.

Warwick Hood

Warwick Hood, designer of the Australian challenger, *Dame Pattie* for the 1967 match, is an unlucky man. He was unlucky first of all for his boat to have to meet Bus Mosbacher sailing *Intrepid* in the year when *Intrepid* demolished everything before her. *Intrepid* lost only one race that year and that one only because her navigator went to the wrong mark in an early trial race on Long Island Sound. In every other race all summer long she took *Weatherly, American Eagle, Columbia,* and *Constellation* into camp, usually by wide margins. She won convincingly in light air but was even more impressive on the few days there was heavy air.

Hood was unlucky also that the gamble he made in designing *Dame Pattie* to be at her best in light air backfired. It was a logical, perhaps even sensible gamble but there were fresh winds, though not really strong ones, in all four races of the match, and *Dame Pattie* was overpowered. In the heaviest weather, which came in the first race which started in eighteen knots of wind, she lost by five minutes fifty-eight seconds, but in the other three the margins were all about three and a half minutes. In the last race when the wind died from twelve knots at the start to eight at the finish *Dame Pattie* actually gained on one leg and held virtually even on another. If it had been

Warwick Hood, designer of the unlucky 1967 Australian challenger, Dame Pattie.

an all light air series, I still do not think she could have handled *Intrepid* but she would surely have been closer. As it was, in weather generally not to her liking, *Dame Pattie* lost to *Intrepid* by slightly lesser margins than the other American contenders had throughout the summer. Without question Hood had designed a good Twelve, capable of beating any Twelve Meter then afloat except the one she had to beat in the match.

Warwick Hood, who was 35 years old when he designed *Dame Pattie*, is a quiet, modest, almost self-effacing man. He will not go down in history as one of the great America's Cup designers, but he deserves to be remembered as a far better one than *Dame Pattie*'s record might lead one to conclude.

Britton Chance

Britton Chance deserves inclusion among the list of designers of boats which raced for the America's Cup because his redesign of *Intrepid* for the 1970 match was so complete that, though originally an Olin Stephens design, when Brit got through with her she was truly his own. Something in the neighborhood of $300,000 was spent modifying the lovely *Intrepid* of 1967. Her keel was replaced with a much shorter one to reduce wetted surface. Her stern sections were filled out and displacement increased. And her deck layout was changed drastically.

Brit should not be too heavily criticized for the fact that these changes probably slowed *Intrepid* down. This was the year that all the American designers went too far in exploring the upper limits of the International Rule. Olin Stephens started with a new design after extensive tank testing as did Charley Morgan, designer of *Heritage.* Yet, Brit Chance's redesign was clearly the cream of a rather sour lot. The handwriting was on the wall when the venerable *Weatherly* pressed them in several races and even won a few. All the new boats accelerated slowly, made leeway in light air until speed was built up and required a real breeze before they began to feel lively. But Brit Chance had designed a faster boat than Olin, with both of them having explored the same type of design. In the final trials, *Intrepid* beat *Valiant* in six out of the seven races they sailed against each other. She was the only American boat of that year that could have beaten *Gretel.*

Chance's weakness, however, was his lack of objectivity in recognizing that while *Intrepid* was the best of the American boats she was no great shakes. With his already boundless self-confidence buoyed by this success, he must have believed himself infallible because four years later he created in *Mariner* one of the most radical (and disasterous) Twelves of all time.

While Olin recognized that he had goofed in 1970 and got back on the track by creating the more conventional but superlative *Courageous* and revamping *Intrepid* to an even higher standard than that achieved in her initial year, Chance plowed off boldly into unchartered waters. The most unusual feature of *Mariner* was a squared-off flat section at the after end of her run below the waterline. Tank tests had indicated to Chance that this increased sailing length and that, contrary to what one might have expected, it did not increase drag. What he had overlooked was the scale effect which made it efficient on a small model but which did not work on a full-sized Twelve. At a speed of twenty knots it might work but in light air it was disasterous; disasterous also at a Twelve's top speed of eleven knots. Brit was so sure of himself that the same type "fastback" stern was affixed to *Valiant* which was serving as *Mariner*'s trial horse. As a result they lost their yardstick and by beating *Valiant* in early brushes developed false confidence. I remember viewing her afterbody with horror on the day *Mariner* was christened. It just did not seem possible to me that such a shape

could do anything but create turbulence and drag. Early trial sails revealed her causing all sorts of fuss and pulling a stern wave, instead of leaving a smooth wake. *Mariner*'s skipper, Ted Turner, was customarily outspoken (and correct) in evaluating this radical design feature by exclaiming: "My God, Brit, don't you know that even turds are tapered."

Through it all Brit maintained an air of supreme confidence. He even seemed unconvinced after *Courageous* annihilated *Mariner* in the N.Y.Y.C. spring regatta June 1 and 2. I couldn't believe how much faster we were than both *Mariner* and *Valiant* with their "fastback" sterns. It was obvious to us that *Mariner* was so much slower that nothing but drastic surgery could make her a contender. Chance, however, blamed her losses on the fact that Turner was sailing poorly, wiggling too much, and not keeping her in the groove. This did not make him very popular with *Mariner*'s skipper or crew but more important it prevented them from making modifications. Instead, *Mariner* went to Newport unmodified to participate in the preliminary trials commencing 24 June. It was only after she got trounced in that series that she went back to the builder's yard where at great expense her "fastback" was removed and a new underbody designed. This caused her to miss the July trials and the valuable experience they provide. When *Mariner* returned for the final trials in August she was improved, but by that time *Courageous* and *Intrepid* were in fine tune and *Mariner* never won a single race except when paired against *Valiant.*

Three weeks had been lost when Chance was too stubborn or too blind to admit after those two early races in June that *Mariner* and not her crew was hopelessly outclassed. Had she been modified immediately she could have shaken down in the July trials and have been far more ready for the final trials in August. Even as modified I do not feel she could have ever been the equal of either *Courageous* or *Intrepid* but the delay in making changes made her cause completely hopeless.

Britton Chance is in many respects a fine designer, as well as a good sailor. His father was an Olympic gold medalist and Brit has also been a highly successful skipper in keen competition. He designed a number of outstanding 5.5 Meters and more than a few fine ocean racers. His Achilles heel is an inability to recognize or to admit his mistakes when he makes them. In consequence he pursues blind alleys too long. I remember a discussion about boats with Brit when we were flying back home from London following the I.Y.R.U. meetings. I admit to being no designer, admit to not having Brit's scientific mind, but I will not admit to not knowing something about boats. Whenever I expressed an opinion different from his, Brit then gave me the Word as if from on high. I feel Britton Chance is a highly intelligent, perhaps even brilliant man. Should he ever learn that he is not always right, he could still develop into a brilliant designer. He is plenty smart. All he needs are some "street smarts."

Bob Miller

Bob Miller, designer of *Southern Cross* in 1974 and codesigner with Johan Valentijn of *Australia* the 1977 challenger, is one of the finest sailors ever to design an America's Cup challenger. He has been Australian Champion

in the Soling class (and twice on Australia's Olympic team) and he has raced everything from dinghies to ocean racers. It is his instinctive feel for boats, his constant involvement with boats, and not book learning which has made him a great designer. His formal education stopped at an early stage because he hated school, was bad at math, and so he quit. He feels this is perhaps an advantage because it forced him to learn yacht design by looking at boats, sailing good boats, and instinctively concluding what features make them go. In so many respects he is like that great American sailor and designer, the late C. Raymond Hunt. Both Miller and Hunt had little book learning, both made mistakes occasionally, but both had great empathy with the sea. They are both innovative and both have created some outstanding designs.

I first met Bob when I was in England for the 1973 Admiral's Cup series. Miller's designs, *Apollo II* and *Ginkho* were members of the Australian team and in my book were the two fastest boats there. He is a fun guy to be with. He is big, warm, good humored, amusing, and not a bit stuck on himself. But you know immediately that he knows what he is talking about.

He first got into the business by becoming a sailmaker and a very good one and then became a designer. One of his more recent designs is the maxi-ocean racer *Ballyhoo* which beat the great *Kialoa* in the races for the California Cup and the San Francisco Perpetual Trophy. She also won the China Seas Race and took fourteen hours off the previous record in the Around the State Race, a circumnavigation of the Hawaiian Islands.

In *Southern Cross* he came up with a fine Twelve, probably the fastest Twelve ever on a reach. She was innovative in having an articulated rudder, a feature which may or may not have helped her. Out of water she looked fast and on the race course she lived up to her looks.

She had the misfortune of sailing against *Courageous,* the misfortune also of trying to best Dennis Conner at the start. Still in both of the first two races she was leading halfway up the first weather leg. Tactical errors did her in each time and she rounded the first mark behind. In the second race which she lost by only one minute eleven seconds she had her best chance. Had she not overstood she could have rounded first and on the reaches she proved faster.

After two losses, at least one of which could have been a win, the brain trust on *Southern Cross* panicked and made a number of unfortunate changes in the sails they used. She then lost the next two by wide margins, but it is my feeling that with everything right *Southern Cross* was very nearly the equal of *Courageous* and capable of beating *Courageous* had she been the better sailed boat.

Ben Lexcen and Johan Valentijn

No need to say anything about Ben Lexcen because he is really Bob Miller. For some unexplained reason he had his name changed legally to Lexcen, probably because of some legal reason, though no one seems to know. What I do know is that if you are walking up the street behind him and call "Hello, Ben" nothing happens, but if you say "Hi, Bob" he turns

immediately. In any event, he remains the same fine bloke he always was.

For the 1977 challenge he teamed with Johan Valentijn. Valentijn's qualifications complement Miller's to a "T". He graduated in naval architecture and marine engineering from the Technical Academy at Haarlem in the Netherlands. And unlike Miller or Lexcen (take your choice) his air and demeanor is studious. He had one other great thing going for him. For five years he was employed at Sparkman & Stephens and he was familiar with the lines of *Courageous.*

Australia could easily have been an exact copy of *Courageous* but to the new design team's credit she wasn't. True, there is a family resemblence below the waterline (albeit with changes) but above the water she is distinctly different. Her freeboard is a full six inches lower. That in itself would make her faster but reduced freeboard imposes a penalty under the Rule which can be offset only from reduction in waterline length and/or sail area. In *Australia*'s case the waterline length was reduced. It is interesting to note that Olin Stephens's latest Twelve Meter, *Freedom,* also has reduced free-board, almost precisely that of *Australia's.*

In the match, *Australia* proved fast. She gained on the downwind legs but was always behind at the start and at the first mark. Thereafter she lost little ground. It is my feeling that if the crews and jibs had been swapped the Americans could have defended successfully sailing *Australia.* I do not mean to imply she is inherently faster than *Courageous* (I doubt it but I am not sure) but I do know her jibs were god-awful and she was not sailed as well as *Courageous.* In short, she is a fine Twelve. Just how fine we will perhaps learn in 1980 because she is coming back.

Coming back, also, is Johan Valentijn. He has taken out French citizenship and is the designer of *France III.* Where there is a will there is a way and Baron Bich and Valentijn sure have the will. The conditions require that the designer be a citizen of the challenging nation and such was the America's Cup fever of both the Baron and Valentijn that this was taken care of. We will have to wait a bit to see whether they will have succeeded in finding the way to win the America's Cup.

Chapter VIII
The Famous Protests

The long history of the America's Cup has been marred by few protests but there were zingers in both of the two closest matches. Had they been decided in favor of the challenger the Cup could have gone overseas.

In the fourth race of the 1934 match *Endeavour* protested *Rainbow* for two alleged violations, one after the preparatory signal, the other on the second leg. In the first incident Sopwith claimed that *Rainbow* "while overtaking yacht" balked *Endeavour* and forced her to bear away to avoid a collision. The second incident occurred after rounding the first mark, Sopwith claiming that as *Rainbow* was passing *Endeavour* to windward she failed to respond to *Endeavour*'s luff and that *Endeavour* was forced to bear away to avoid a very serious collision.

Unfortunately, neither protest was heard by the New York Yacht Club Race Committee which was also the protest committee. They were not for the good and proper reason that the rules then as now specified that "a protest on the score of breach of rules occurring during a race must be signified by *showing a flag conspicuously* in the main rigging of the protesting yacht *at the first reasonable opportunity* and when passing the sailing committee unless the competitor has no knowledge of the facts justifying the protest until after the conclusion of the Race. Failure to observe this rule will debar a competing yacht from bringing the incident to the notice of the committee."

Note particularly the words *"at the first reasonable opportunity."* You might not like this rule. In fact I do not, since it prevents a guilty yacht from being disqualified if the innocent one is tardy in flying a protest flag. BUT IT IS A RULE, IT IS SPECIFIC AND WHETHER THEY LIKE IT OR NOT A PROTEST COMMITTEE MUST BE BOUND BY IT.

It is a matter of uncontested fact that *Endeavour*'s flag was not displayed until about three hours after the occurrence of the first alleged foul and nearly two hours after the occurrence of the second alleged foul. Sopwith was tardy because the frequent practice abroad was to display a flag only when next passing the Committee boat. Their rule specified that the flag must be displayed "at the earliest possible moment and when next passing the Committee boat." They often sailed a course two or three times around and tended to neglect the "and" in their requirement and considered that they had fullfilled the requirement of the rule if the flag was displayed when next passing the Committee boat.

Sopwith, in learning that the committee would not hear his protest, wrote as follows: "I regret to note that your committee refuses to hear *Endeavour*'s protest of yesterday owing to my not having complied with a very trivial technical formality regarding the time my protest flag was flying." I sympathize with his point of view but I do not agree with it. The rule under which he was racing was specific and he did not comply with it.

The general public and the press, however, were all on Sopwith's side and felt that the New York Yacht Club had acted in a high-handed manner.

What they did not know or chose to overlook, was the fact that the Race Committee had seen the first incident at close hand, had made notes on it, and subsequently had the added evidence of a series of photos and were convinced that in the first incident *Endeavour* was dead wrong. They expected *Rainbow* to hoist a protest flag but Mike Vanderbilt chose not to. In the words of the committee, printed later in the club's records for that year's racing, the committee stated:

> We are reliably informed that the international character of the race alone prevented *Rainbow* from protesting at the start, it having been agreed between Harold S. Vanderbilt and the America's Cup Committee, prior to the commencement of the races, that as a matter of policy protests should be avoided.
>
> Your committee were unanimously of the opinion that in the event of a hearing held by them they would have had to disqualify *Endeavour* for having failed to observe the Racing Rule which reads: "When both yachts have the wind free on different sides, and neither can claim the rights of a yacht being overtaken, the yacht which has the wind on the port side shall keep out of the way of the other."

They did not buy Sopwith's claim that *Rainbow* was overtaking and anyone studying the photos of the incident, as I have, would have to agree. The committee also stated that: "It seemed impossible to your Committee that the taking of evidence at a hearing could cause us to materially modify the views formed as a result of our own very clear observation and now substantiated by photographs of the incident."

It is for the above reason that the committee decided not to institute an investigation of its own into the incidents covered by the protests. They had the power to do so under the rule of the era which read: "Should it come to the knowledge of the Race Committee, or should they have reasonable grounds to believe that a competitor in a race has in any way infringed these rules, they shall have the power to disqualify such competitor without protest . . . after a hearing."

They did not utilize this power simply because had they done so they would have had to disqualify *Endeavour* for the incident which occurred before the start.

None of this explanation was given at the time nor did it appear until months later. Instead the committee suffered in silence and based their case solely on the fact that Sopwith had flown his flag too late, which in fact he had. I am certain, however, that had the committee not viewed the first incident so clearly and been so sure that *Endeavour* was wrong it would have instituted an investigation of its own into the second incident. Nowadays if they did so and *Endeavour* had been found to be in the right, *Rainbow* would have been disqualified under the second incident, *Endeavour* under the first one, and the race would have been resailed. But under the rules in force in 1934 if a yacht was disqualified for an incident early in a race, it was impossible to disqualify the other yacht for committing a foul later in the same race. That is not the way it is now but that was the law of the sea in those days. In the committee's own words, published months later:

> *Endeavour*'s second protest, covering the luffing incident which occurred after rounding the first mark, could never have come before your committee since we would have had to disqualify one of the yachts prior to the start (see case of *Lena* versus *Countess,* Report of the New York Yacht Club Race Committee, 1924).

The committee then went on to write for posterity:

> Your committee believed it would serve no useful purposes to hold a hearing which, in its opinion, could only have resulted in the disqualification of *Endeavour* and furthermore that to institute a proceeding on its own initiative where in the language of the rule it had 'reasonable grounds to believe' that the challenger had fouled the defender and not the defender the challenger, and the defender had not protested, would be regarded by many as indicating an advocacy of the *Rainbow* on the part of a committee whose sole duty was to enforce impartially the agreed rules of the Race.

These words may sound self-serving but when one considers that the rules of that day would not have allowed a consideration of the second incident since by then one of the yachts would have been already disqualified they must be accepted as an honest and accurate statement. I feel this also because I know the chairman of the committee, Edmund Lang, and my dad knew him intimately. He was one straight guy!

But even though the committee could not look into it, what was the story on the second incident? Was Sopwith right or wrong? While we will never know for sure, I am inclined to feel he was right. What is known is that when *Rainbow* was passing *Endeavour* on a reach *Endeavour* luffed and *Rainbow* did not respond. What is also known is that *Endeavour* then bore off to avoid a serious collision.

There was no mast-line rule in those days to determine when luffing rights were lost. Instead a leeward yacht maintained luffing rights as long as her luff would result in her boat striking the windward yacht forward of her leeward shrouds. To be sure who was right a collision would have had to occur—a pretty risky business in boats the size of J-boats.

Knowing Mike Vanderbilt as I do, I am convinced he felt *Rainbow* was far enough past by the time *Endeavour* luffed so that she would have struck *Rainbow* abaft the shrouds. Most of his afterguard felt the same way, but remember that those on the windward boat in such a situation are apt to indulge in a bit of wishful thinking. They want so much for the leeward yacht to have lost luffing rights that they are apt to talk themselves into truly believing that she has, even though in fact she has not lost them. Just the reverse is true of those on the leeward yacht.

But one member of *Rainbow*'s afterguard felt differently. That was Sherman Hoyt who was stationed at the leeward shrouds. He shouted in vain for Mike to come up. In his book, *Sherman Hoyt's Memoirs,* published many years later, Sherman is vague on this point, perhaps out of loyalty to Vanderbilt. But he was not vague in talking to me about it. He told me point blank that he believed that if *Endeavour* had pursued her luff she would have struck *Rainbow* right at the shrouds, perhaps even a bit forward of them. This was expressed to me even more definitely by Frank Murdoch, one of *Endeavour*'s crew members, some twenty years after the incident. Frank is convinced that *Endeavour* had not lost luffing rights and would have hit *Rainbow* forward of the shrouds.

Sir Ralph Gore, the British observer on *Rainbow,* was of the opinion that *Endeavour* probably had lost luffing rights though he was not sure. What he was sure of was that the proper course of action on *Rainbow*'s part would have been to respond to the luff and then protest if she felt *Endeavour* had luffed too late. With this I agree.

It is risky to surmise who was right and who was wrong without the benefit of a full hearing to determine all the facts, and such a hearing (quite properly under the rules of that day) was never held. But even though it is risky, I am of the view that if a hearing had been held *Rainbow* would have been found in the wrong. The facts would have been inconclusive, with everyone on *Endeavour* claiming that she never lost luffing rights and those on *Rainbow* claiming she had. The committee, faced with this difference of opinion would then be apt to disqualify *Rainbow* for not responding, one fact that all agree with. As stated earlier, it would not have mattered in any case since prior to that, one boat (almost certainly *Endeavour*) would have been disqualified under the prestart incident. But if they had then been sailing under the rules in effect in 1980, my guess is that the committee would have initiated action on both alleged violations, and would have thrown out *Endeavour* under the first incident and *Rainbow* under the second one. Had that been the case the race would have to be resailed and the score would have remained two races to one in favor of *Endeavour* instead of being two to two. In that event *Endeavour* might still have pulled out the match because she was the faster boat and even after losing the next two races might have come back to win two more and take the Cup.

It is a pity that all this had to happen in the closest match in America's Cup history but it did happen. Still the protest committee acted in the only way it possibly could and at this writing, forty-six years later, Tom Sopwith, who is still hale and hearty, bears no grudge and instead remembers the 1934 match as one of the great experiences of his life.

One good thing did come out of these protests. I am confident they had a big bearing on getting the luffing rule changed to today's far better version and also in sparking the rule change which retains a yacht's rights after she has committed a foul earlier in the race, including the right to protest the other yacht and have her disqualified for a later violation in the same race.

The other big protest occurred thirty-six years later in the 1970 match between *Gretel II* and *Intrepid.* This one did come to a hearing and did result in the disqualification of *Gretel II* from the second race after she had won it on the race course.

There has never been a more significant protest yet never one in which the facts were easier to determine since it happened right at the start, in full view of the committee. The facts were further corroborated by a series of aerial and sea-level photos.

Here is what happened. Both yachts were approaching the weather end of the starting line with *Gretel II* to leeward and attempting to close the gap between herself and the Committee boat. *Intrepid* was in a barging situation on *Gretel II*'s weather quarter and had no right to ask for room. But if there was room for her to pass between *Gretel II* and the Committee boat without illegally forcing *Gretel II* to bear off to provide it, then she would commit no foul. There is nothing illegal about barging if there is sufficient room but it is a ticklish situation. Until the starting gun fired *Gretel II* could sail as high as she wanted, including luffing head to wind and, knowing this, Ficker held back and waited to see if there would be sufficient room. He knew that once the starting gun fired *Gretel II* could no longer sail above a close-hauled course to close the gap between her and the Committee boat. With a few seconds still to go he determined that when *Gretel II* did bear off to such a course after the starting gun fired there would be sufficient room between *Gretel II* and the Committee boat for *Intrepid* to sail through without fouling either and without forcing *Gretel II* to bear off below a close-hauled course. Hence he trimmed in, built speed, and charged for the narrow gap, feeling it would become just wide enough once *Gretel II* bore off to a close-hauled course with the starting gun. It was a gutsy call but faint heart never won a boat race and he was confident that enough room (but just enough) would be there.

As the gun fired *Gretel II* was just under two lengths short of the line with *Intrepid* almost overlapped on her weather quarter and traveling almost twice as fast. To Ficker's astonishment when the gun fired *Gretel II,* instead of bearing off to a close hauled course, continued to luff. I was 200 feet away on one of the privileged vessels allowed inside the spectator fleet and I exclaimed to a keen sailing friend I was standing next to: "The gun has gone and *Gretel* is luffing higher instead of bearing off". He agreed and we could both see her sails, both main and jib, luffing badly even though they were trimmed in tight. *Intrepid* was now committed, she kept going, swept past *Gretel II* and all the time she did so (and this was some fifteen seconds after the gun) *Gretel*'s sails kept shaking and we could see no alteration of her course to leeward. Finally as they passed the committee boat, with *Gretel II* nearly head to wind and *Intrepid* tight reaching, *Gretel*'s stem struck *Intrepid*'s leeward quarter.

Gretel II was now nearly dead in the water because she had been luffing so long and *Intrepid* sped out to a huge early lead. *Gretel II* proved so fast and sailed such a masterful race thereafter that despite the early deficit she went on to win. I remember, even though I wanted *Intrepid* to win, feeling sorry for Hardy for losing a race through a silly foul which he otherwise deserved to win. There was no question in my mind, based on what I had seen from close hand, that *Gretel II* had fouled and would lose the protest.

The pertinent rule reads as follows:

> SECTION E—Rules of Exception and Special Application
> 42.1(e) When overlapped when approaching the starting line to start, a leeward yacht shall be under no obligation to give any windward yacht room to pass to leeward of a starting mark surrounded by navigable water; but, after the starting signal, a leeward yacht shall not deprive a windward yacht of room at such a mark by sailing either above the first mark or above close-hauled.

I was at *Gretel*'s dock when she came in, both to congratulate Jim Hardy for a well sailed race and at the same time to commiserate with him about the unfortunate foul.

I was one of the first people to talk to him and was surprised to find him without a care in the world and ebullient about his victory. When I lamented the foul, he replied instantly, "No problem, we will win that too." I was so surprised by his confidence that I asked if he had luffed after the

This sequence of photos shows why **Gretel II** *was disqualified. In photo #1 the starting signal has just been hoisted (see smoke from starting gun). Hereafter* **Gretel II** *can sail no higher than close hauled to deprive* **Intrepid** *of room between her and the Committee boat.*

Photo #3 shows the moment of contact with **Gretel II** *still sailing well above a close-hauled course. Note the Committee looking closely at the action.*

In photo #2 Gretel *is luffing almost head to wind. Note how much her sails are luffing.* Intrepid *having expected* Gretel II *to bear off keeps going for the line.*

In this photo Gretel II*, her speed spent by luffing and from being blanketed is almost dead in the water.* Intrepid *appears home free but* Gretel II *gained on the fifth leg and finished more than a minute ahead, only to lose through disqualification for the foul of the century.*

starting gun had fired. "Sure," he replied, "we kept luffing to squeeze Ficker out." To be absolutely sure, I repeated the question. "Did you luff after the gun had fired?" Again he said, "Yes, we kept luffing." Then he added something to the effect, "We wanted to nail him good and prove he was barging."

I have kept this conversation in confidence for ten years, and especially during the ensuing day that the race committee was deliberating the protest. The chairman, Dev Barker, was a good friend of mine and I was fearful he might ask my view of the incident and I wanted no part of supplying information I had gained from Jim Hardy in a friendly and casual conversation. I realized it would cook his goose, and while I knew it should be cooked, I did not relish the idea of being the master chef. Dev could have asked my opinion because I was a member of the International Yacht Racing Union's Racing Rules Committee, had written a book on the interpretation of the racing rules, and was considered somewhat of an authority.

Actually the committee needed to consult no one since they had seen the incident at close hand and they knew the rules cold. But to leave no stones unturned they did confirm their own judgment by talking to Gregg Bemis, chairman of the I.Y.R.U. Racing Rules Committee. It was overkill to check in this manner, but they wanted to be absolutely sure before rendering a decision.

After the most careful deliberation they rendered their decision, disqualifying *Gretel II.* The pertinent part of their decision read as follows:

> "Both yachts were approaching the starting line to start within the context of Rule 42.1(e). Prior to the starting signal, *Gretel II* was under no obligation to give *Intrepid* room to pass to leeward of the Committee boat. After the starting signal, however, *Gretel II* acquired an obligation, as soon as the yachts were overlapped, not to deprive *Intrepid* of room to pass on the required side of the committee boat by sailing above close-hauled.
>
> Had *Gretel II* fulfilled her obligation to fall off to a close-hauled course under Rule 42.1(e), *Intrepid* would have had room to pass between *Gretel II* and the Committee boat.

Press conferences are an integral part of the America's Cup. This one, in which I am serving as M.C., shows Dev Barker reading the fateful decision disqualifying Gretel II *in the second race of 1970.*

Therefore, *Gretel II* is disqualified for infringement of Rule 42.1(e).

That succinct and accurate decision should have ended the matter but it did not. The Yacht Club was deluged with telegrams and phone calls from people who knew little of the racing rules but who still accused the club of foul play. One such came from the Princeton University football coach who did not know the bow of a boat from her stern but who like many others still felt emboldened to castigate the Club for foul play.

And the Aussies, or rather Frank Packer, chairman of the *Gretel II* syndicate, did not take the decision lying down. Instead Packer attempted to reopen the case, citing rules which had no bearing on the case in hand. All such attempts were listened to carefully and then dismissed on logical grounds. Still the furor continued.

At this time, after another race had been sailed I asked Bill Fesq, navigator of *Gretel II,* how he felt about the disqualification. He told me they then knew they were wrong. "Will you so state at a postrace press conference?" I asked. "Sure," he replied, "but not until the end of the series." He indicated that to do so sooner would tend to undermine Martin Visser, their starting helmsman who was at *Gretel II*'s wheel when the foul occurred.

Yet at the end of the series neither Hardy nor Fesq did make such a statement. They did compliment the Yacht Club for behaving in a gentlemanly fashion but they never did admit they were wrong.

Strangely, in all the years since, neither Hardy nor Fesq have so admitted. In fact, a number of years later they appear to have talked themselves into believing they had a case after all. Both are honorable and forthright men and I can conclude only that they wanted so very much to be right that they convinced themselves, albeit with no logical reason, that they were right. The fact of the matter is that at the time of the foul they were ignorant of the right-of-way rule which required *Gretel* to fall off to a close-hauled course as soon as the starting gun had gone! That ignorance cost them the race and even conceivably the Cup itself.

The pity of it all, from their standpoint, is that if they had just sailed their own boat instead of trying to make *Intrepid* commit a foul they would have won that race and perhaps the series. They protested in race one also, claiming that *Intrepid* had been guilty of an opposite tack violation. In truth, it appeared more likely that *Gretel II* was guilty of balking in an attempt to nail *Intrepid* while she was on port tack, but taking every proper action to keep clear. Since no collision occurred neither yacht was disqualified, but had there been one, *Gretel II,* on starboard tack, might well have been thrown out for balking *Intrepid* while the latter was fullfilling her obligation to keep clear. The handwriting was on the wall that Visser was out for blood. The same type of aggressive tactics in the second race proved to be his undoing.

There is one other anecdote regarding *Gretel*'s disqualification which now with the passage of time is, I feel, appropriate to tell. It was after another race had been sailed but before the series had concluded. I was viewing the match from the same boat as the America's Cup committee. I noticed a meeting going on between the committee, the then commodore of the club, plus several immediate past commodores. About ten minutes after the meeting had been in progress I was invited to join the group. I was then President of the North American Yacht Racing Union and it was in this official capacity that my advice was sought. Without indicating their own view on the matter, they informed me that they had been discussing the advisability of canceling the second race and ordering it resailed. They did say they agreed with the Race Committee decision to disqualify *Gretel II* but then asked how I felt about canceling the race in the interest of harmony and future good relations between nations competing for the America's Cup. It took me all of five seconds to blurt out that such might promote goodwill but that it would also make it appear that the Yacht Club had erred in the first place, whereas in fact it had made the only possible decision under the racing rules. I further stated that it would make a mockery of rule enforcement and would establish a very bad precedent. They thanked me for my opinion and then opined that they had come to precisely the same conclusion but wanted the view of the head of the national governing body on yacht racing. I mention this only to demonstrate how far the New York Yacht Club bent over backwards in the interest of being fair and impartial. They actually were considering nullifying a decision they knew to be right. I hope these gentlemen do not take exception to my divulging this conversation ten years after the event. It is a story which I feel needs to be told to offset all the unwarranted vilification the club had received from a number of bleeding hearts who knew nothing about what really had happened or the pertinent rule which governed the situation.

One most fortunate thing evolved from this unfortunate protest. After the 1970 match and for all future matches the protest committee has been and will continue to be composed of an international jury, with no members from the same nation as the defender or the challenger. Beppe Croce, president of the International Yacht Racing Union, was chairman of the jury for the 1974 and 1977 matches and will be again for the 1980 one. The result will be fair decisions more quickly arrived at, and decisions which will be accepted with less criticism than heretofore. Not better decisions, not worse ones. Just the same correct ones, but fairer to both parties and *far less subject to criticism.* In the past the New York Yacht Club has leaned over backwards to be fair, leaned so very far as to risk being unfair to their own boat. For example, prior to the start of the first race for the 1934 match the New York Yacht Club Race Committee noticed that *Endeavour* was having difficulty hoisting her mainsail after the course signals had been set. Despite the fact that the conditions of the match called for yachts to be ready to start at the agreed-upon time, they postponed the start long enough for *Endeavour* to be ready. I approve of their action but it certainly gave *Endeavour* a break. And you can bet your bottom dollar that if it had been *Rainbow* which was having difficulty getting ready for the start, *the starting time would not have been postponed.* Or if it had been, the Club would still be hearing repercussions of favoritism. Far better to have an international body make such decisions and render decisions on protests. The same decisions will be rendered. The only difference will be in their more ready acceptance by the competitors, by yachtsmen everywhere, and by the public at large which become overnight experts on things they know nothing about when the America's Cup is on the line. The only thing which I criticize the New York Yacht Club about is why they took so long to realize how vital it is to have an international jury rather than their own Race Committee to decide protests. It took the *Gretel–Intrepid* protest and the ensuing hue and cry from their perfectly correct decision to wake them up.

Chapter IX
The Role of the Selection Committee

William H. "Bill" Taylor wrote in the September, 1930 issue of *Yachting*: "There is probably no less enviable a task connected with the defense of the America's Cup than that of the Selection Committee." Bill is probably the most noted yachting reporter of all time, having received a Pulitzer Prize for his reporting on the 1934 match, the only sports writer to receive this award. And in this statement he was as usual dead right. The Selection Committee, otherwise knows as the America's Cup Committee, has an awesome burden to select the yacht which in their opinion has the best chance to defend the Cup successfully. Sometimes it is easy, as in the case of *Ranger* in 1937 and *Intrepid* in 1967. These two so dominated the trial races that the Committee's job was superflous. No other selection was conceivably possible.

In the majority of years the winning yacht selects herself by dominating the final trials. But on a few occasions it comes right down to the wire. In that instance only those on the selected yacht are happy, the losers feel that with just a few more races they could turn the tide. And it is a sobering and difficult task to tell a skipper and his crew who have been in close contention for several months that a decision has been made to select an opponent which has only a slightly better record, or conceivably a worse record over the course of the full summer of racing.

I know the feeling because I was privileged to be a member of the 1977 America's Cup Committee and it was not easy to tell the crews of *Enterprise* and *Independence* that they were through and that *Courageous* had been selected. *Enterprise* in particular took it hard, believing that with just a bit more time they could turn the tide, this despite the fact that *Courageous* had dominated not only the final selection trial races but most of the prior races. I can thus imagine how very hard it would be in a really tight series.

There is a feeling which has persisted for many years that the Selection Committee is partial to a New York area boat. I know that in the Boston, Marblehead area there at least used to be a feeling that the decks were stacked against them, a feeling which perhaps was engendered by the selection of *Rainbow* over *Yankee* in 1934, despite the fact that *Yankee* won far more races through the course of the summer.

I suspect also that the crew of *Intrepid* in 1974 felt that the Selection Committee was partial to *Courageous* as a home town favorite. But having served on the Committee, and having learned how they reason and the criteria for selection, I can state most categorically that the only thing they are concerned with is finding the boat which in their view will make the strongest possible defense. She can come from Boston, Seattle, California, or Timbuktoo and her chances are precisely even with a boat hailing, say, from Long Island Sound.

The Committee might hate one skipper's guts but if he can win the trials, especially the final trials, and if his boat shows the all-around ability deemed so essential for a defender, he will be selected. The Cup Committee feels an awesome responsibility to pick the right boat, and logic, not emotion, is the only criteria they use.

I knew and liked all three skippers in the 1977 campaign. Still I had a particular skipper I was rooting for. Other members of the Committee, I am

The 1977 America's Cup Committee which selected Courageous *to defend. Left to right: Jim Michael, Bob Bavier, Harry Anderson, chairman George Hinman, Clayton Ewing, Briggs Cunningham and Bus Mosbacher.*

sure, had their favorite but none of us tipped our hand. All deliberations were based on race results and results in various wind strengths and never did I detect any member arguing in a partial way for some skipper who I suspected was his personal favorite or against some other he might have been less keen for in a personal sense. Keep in mind that no Committee member wants to be the first to select a loser of the America's Cup.

The selection, in my view, is based on a few key points. First, the defender must prove to be a well-rounded boat which is not going to lie down and die in either light or heavy air. One boat might win almost all the time in heavy air, and if the trials have a predominance of strong winds she could well have the best record. Let's say, however, that in light air this boat is a real dog, while there is another boat which loses very narrowly in a breeze but dominates in light. The latter boat is much the best bet. Challengers might go all out and gamble with a one weather boat and then hope that the match is sailed in that weather. It could be a way to beat us, but the Selection Committee prefers not to gamble and instead to select a well-rounded boat.

For example, in 1962 Ted Hood's *Nefertiti* had a record of eleven wins, one loss in the July trials. She beat *Weatherly* in three out of the four times they met. But all but one of these races were sailed in winds over eleven knots, most of them over fifteen knots. Her one light air win was over *Easterner,* the weak boat of the group. Although *Weatherly*'s record in these trials was six wins and five losses, one of her wins was against *Nefertiti* in fourteen knots and she had a close loss against *Columbia* in nineteen knots. In short, she proved to be no dog in fresh air.

In the final trials seven of the nine races were in winds under eleven knots, and *Weatherly*'s record was eight wins and one loss. Furthermore, she beat *Nefertiti* in four of the five races they met. Of equal importance was a win over *Columbia* in twenty knots, again proving she was no slouch in a fresh breeze. *Nefertiti*'s only win over *Weatherly* in the final trials was in a twenty-five knot wind.

Weatherly did two things to earn selection. She peaked in the final trials which are the most important ones. Secondly, she won big in light air, won several medium air races, one heavy air race and was never completely out of it. For the summer her record was fourteen wins, six losses while *Nefertiti*'s was fifteen wins and six losses. Still it was not a difficult decision to pick *Weatherly*.

And it is fortunate that she was picked! In the match against *Gretel,* four of the races were in light to moderate air (ten knots, nine to twelve knots, and two in winds of eight to ten knots). *Weatherly* won these four but one of them by a scant twenty-six seconds. The only race she lost was the second one in winds ranging from twenty to twenty-five knots. Even in that one she came close, leading at the first mark by twelve seconds, at the second one by fourteen, until *Gretel* swept by on the last reach to win by

The Selection Committee got this close to the action during the 1977 trials. We are on the power boat to the right, watching Enterprise, *followed closely by her tender.*

132

forty-seven seconds. Had *Nefertiti* been the defender she probably would have won the second race, but she could very possibly have lost the other four.

The toughest and most debatable selection was that of *Rainbow* over *Yankee* in 1934. Throughout the summer *Yankee* won eleven of the seventeen races between the two yachts. She beat *Rainbow* in the one race between them in the preliminary trials. She then beat her in all four meetings in the observation trials. The New York Yacht Club Cruise saw *Yankee* beating *Rainbow* in the first five races, making her record against her arch rival at that point ten to zero.

Just when *Rainbow*'s cause seemed hopeless she beat *Yankee* in the last two races on the cruise. Then after losing badly to *Yankee* in their first meeting in the final trials *Rainbow* took the second one by 3:07 and was leading by 37 seconds in the next one when *Yankee* broke a strut and had to retire. *Rainbow* won the ensuing race by 2:21 and the final one by one second. Charlie Adams felt the trials should continue but the Committee felt otherwise. They were impressed by the fact that in the last seven meetings *Rainbow* had won five and was leading in a sixth when *Yankee* broke down. The fact that *Yankee* won only once in the final trials counted more heavily in the Selection Committee's minds than the previous ten straight wins by *Yankee. Rainbow* had come through when she had to. The record in the final trials is the one which really counts.

This is not to mean that the record in the preliminary and observation trials has no bearing on selection. In the event that the final trials were sailed in one weather condition, either all light or all heavy air, even though one boat might dominate she would probably not be selected if she had proved in earlier races to be slow in other conditions. To be selected a boat has to prove her versatility and then, having proved that, she must come through in the final trials.

Despite *Yankee*'s superior summerlong record I feel *Rainbow*'s selection was a sound one. She won when she had to and she kept on improving right through the match against *Endeavour.* Maybe *Yankee* would have beaten *Endeavour,* maybe not. All we know is that *Rainbow* did and I do not buy the garbage that her selection as defender was influenced by the fact that she was the New York boat and *Yankee* the outlander. If *Yankee* had won the last race by one second I am sure there would have been another one. Had she won that one too, my guess is she would have been selected and would have assumed the awesome burden of trying to beat *Endeavour.*

I was personally involved in the other real squeaker confronting the Selection Committee. In the summer of 1974 I was skipper of *Courageous* and we were having a battle royal against *Intrepid.* We split the races between us in the preliminary trials at two apiece but *Intrepid's* record was slightly better than ours in July—four for her and three for us. In the final trials, after losing the first race to *Intrepid, Courageous* won the next four. We were looking good and a few people even had kind remarks for her skipper Bob Bavier. Then we lost the next three to put us all even at four races each and by then I was a bum. By this time it seemed apparent that *Courageous* was very slightly faster than *Intrepid* but that most observers and in particular the Selection Committee felt that *Intrepid* was being sailed better. The logical move in such a situation is to boot the skipper. It was a hard pill for me to swallow after months of racing but I could not quarrel with the wisdom of letting Ted Hood take over.

Several more races were planned but on the ensuing two days the races were postponed for lack of wind. Finally on 2 September, with time for selection absolutely at hand, there was a beautiful eighteen to twenty knot wind. While it was not officially announced ahead of time, everyone knew that the winner of the race would be named as defender. With Ted Hood driving, *Courageous* led at every mark to win by one minute forty-seven seconds and that evening was selected to defend the America's Cup. The two boats had identical records in the final trials, and over the course of the three sets of trials *Intrepid* beat us one more time than we beat her. On the other hand, we never lost a single race to either *Valiant* or *Mariner,* the other two contenders, but *Valiant* did manage one win over *Intrepid.* Therefore the record of the two boats in the trial races was identical and selection was determined on the basis that *Courageous* seemed a slight bit faster and in the hands of Ted Hood was therefore deemed to be a somewhat better bet as defender. Had *Intrepid* won the last race she would have been the only boat ever to defend the Cup in three matches and I have no doubt that she would have defended successfully against *Southern Cross.*

This series of elimination trials probably set a record for personal an-

The Selection Committee congratulates Courageous *crew on their selection. Bob McCullough, head of the* Courageous *syndicate, greets them.*

guish. Ted Turner was replaced as skipper of the real turkey, *Mariner.* I was replaced as skipper of *Courageous* with but one race to go and Jerry Driscoll, skipper of *Intrepid,* came within one race of skippering an America's Cup defender. If you cannot stand up to disappointment then stay out of the America's Cup. This game is for keeps and the Selection Committee, quite properly, does not consider people's feelings in selecting a defender. They want only to keep the Cup here.

Chapter X
The Matches We Nearly Lost: 1920, 1934, 1970

On the afternoon of Thursday, 20 September, 1934, Mike Vanderbilt went below in *Rainbow* to drown his sorrows with coffee and sandwiches. In the preceding few days he had lost two races to the British challenger *Endeavour* by comfortable margins and minutes before had rounded the leeward mark of the third race six minutes thirty-nine seconds behind the blue British boat, which by then had proven she was faster than the defender. To make matters even worse the wind had shifted to make the leg to the finish a near fetch. Following the leader at such a hopeless distance is hardly a time for optimism, and being three races down with just one to go against a faster opponent made Mike conclude that at long last the America's Cup would go overseas. With him was the British observer Sir Ralph Gore, who tried to make Mike feel better by pointing out that it was a faster boat which had done him in and not poor sailing on his part. They also ruminated on the possible benefit to the sport from a victorious challenge. Being honest, objective men they agreed that *Rainbow*'s cause was hopeless. What happened thereafter proved more eloquently than ever before or since in the history of yacht racing the old adage that "a race is never over till the finish."

Up on deck Sherman Hoyt was at *Rainbow*'s wheel, acting for all the world like a race was still on. Up ahead he could see *Endeavour* in a bit of a flat spot and not quite fetching, while *Rainbow* had been lifted so that she could more than fetch. He held as high as possible, even a bit above the finish in hopes of getting into different sailing conditions than the leader. It was still a pretty hopeless situation because when *Endeavour* got the lift she too could fetch or at worst would have to make one small hitch for the finish. With her big lead that was all she required. But Sherman kept holding high in the quite forlorn hope that *Endeavour* might not know exactly where the finish was, would get nervous, and would tack to cover. It was a real long shot but it was the only card they had to play and certainly better than following *Endeavour* directly.

Just as Mike Vanderbilt got back on deck the hoped-for opening happened. Up ahead they could see *Endeavour* slowly coming about! What had been a completely hopeless situation was now just a very bad one and for the first time in the race there was a glimmer of hope. If *Endeavour* tacked on *Rainbow*'s leeward bow she would still win, though by a smaller margin than originally expected. But, if by some miracle *Endeavour* actually elected to cross *Rainbow*'s bow before tacking, not realizing that *Rainbow* was fetching, then there was a real chance.

Mike let Sherman keep the wheel, as was his wont in light air beating, and also because he did not want to disturb a fast improving situation. Sherman kept a full head of steam on *Rainbow* but held as high as he could so as not to tip his hand that she was fetching. It was agonizing as the two boats converged, *Endeavour* actually sailing slightly *away* from the line as she became headed entering *Rainbow*'s lift. It was evident that she could cross by several lengths, but the question was whether she would elect to or would instead tack short in a safe leeward position which would again make *Rainbow*'s cause hopeless.

Not a word was said on *Rainbow* as the two yachts converged. Instead,

Endeavour *leading* Rainbow *in the 1934 match, a match she should have won.*

the crew lay on the leeward deck as though their only thought was how to get *Rainbow* as far to windward as possible just as though they were on a true windward leg. As the time neared when *Endeavour* would have to tack to assume a safe leeward the suspense was almost unbearable. On she came and now it was too late to tack without crossing!

When she did tack finally, she was directly on *Rainbow*'s wind. Sherman bore off slightly, got clear air, and in a matter of minutes had broken through and ahead into a safe leeward position. J-boats can maintain quite astounding speed in light air, traveling several knots faster than the true wind speed once they have built up headway. The resulting apparent wind strength is sufficient to keep them going. But when they tack in light air, boat speed and hence apparent wind strength is reduced and it takes many minutes for them to build their speed back up. That is what happened to *Endeavour.* Although she tacked right on *Rainbow*'s wind, she took so long to rebuild speed in the light air that she could not stay there and could not prevent *Rainbow* from charging through. A few minutes later *Endeavour* had sagged off into *Rainbow*'s backwind and tacked again to clear her air. It was a futile and desperate move which merely put her further behind. *Rainbow* let her go, kept driving for the finish and finally won by three minutes twenty-six seconds. *Rainbow,* making no tacks on the final leg as opposed to *Endeavour*'s four, had gained ten minutes, five seconds.

In Tom Sopwith's defense one can understand his anxiety when he saw *Rainbow* lifted and gaining. A short tack and then a tack back on *Rainbow*'s leeward bow as soon as she was headed would have reduced the lead. But it would have put her in the same wind conditions as *Rainbow,* would have put her in the safe leeward position, and would have retained a victory, albeit a narrow one. But crossing *Rainbow* when *Rainbow* was fetching was an inexcusable error in navigation and tactical judgement.

Now down two races to one, *Rainbow*'s prospects were still dim but not as desperate as the 3–0 score that should have been. Just as important as the mathematical improvement was the psychological one. *Rainbow*'s afterguard and crew got a tremendous lift, while *Endeavour*'s was shaken. Sopwith had sailed well in the first two races as well as the third until making his monumental goof but thereafter everything seemed to go wrong. After the third race *Rainbow* added 4000 pounds of ballast. After the second one *Endeavour* had removed 3360 pounds, a surprising move since she had won the first two quite handily and had shown good speed. Vanderbilt made another and more important move. He added Frank Paine to his afterguard. Paine had been sail trimming officer on *Yankee* and had made *Yankee* excel whenever her parachute spinnaker was up. Paine not only came aboard but brought *Yankee*'s chute with him. He and the sail were so helpful that Mike magnanimously referred to Paine after the match as the "saviour of the America's Cup."

The fourth race was a thriller marred by a protest on the second leg of the triangular course, a protest discussed at length in chapter eight. On the opening beat by careful covering *Rainbow* maintained the slight lead she had achieved at the start. Approaching the mark, however, *Endeavour* was so close on *Rainbow*'s weather quarter that *Rainbow* couldn't tack without fouling. *Endeavour* rounded first by thirty-three seconds but was so slow in setting her genoa that *Rainbow* drove by to windward. As she was passing, *Endeavour* luffed and the protest evolved around Sopwith's claim that Vanderbilt did not respond properly. In any event *Rainbow* swept past, rounded the second mark a minute ahead, and gained another fifteen seconds on the reach to the finish. Frank Paine's sail trimming was credited for her improved reaching ability. The added ballast might well have helped also.

With the score now even and *Rainbow*'s confidence building, she poured it on in the fifth race over a leeward-windward course. The two boats were even at the start but *Rainbow*'s spinnaker broke out smartly while *Endeavour*'s crew seemed to take ages. With Frank Paine calling the spinnaker trim, *Rainbow* kept moving out ahead, gaining so rapidly that even though it ripped halfway down the leg and had to be replaced *Rainbow* still led by four minutes thirty-eight seconds at the leeward mark. *Rainbow*'s lead was gained partly because Sopwith failed to jibe when lifted, while *Rainbow* jibed prior to setting the replacement chute. Still *Rainbow* came close to losing her lead when her boatswain Ben Bruntwith was knocked overboard while releasing the backstay while jibing. Fortunately, Ben had the backstay tail in his hand and although largely underwater for 30 seconds hung on for dear life until the crew could haul him back aboard. Had he lost his grip, *Rainbow* would surely have lost the race as she went back to recover him. On the beat home, *Endeavour* gained thirty-seven seconds but still lost by over four minutes.

In what turned out to be the final race, *Endeavour* should have won but managed to make enough mistakes to more than offset her superior boat

speed. It was a triangular race starting with a reach, then a beat and finally a ten-mile reach to the finish. *Endeavour* led by one minute eight seconds at the first mark but then made a fatal error by starting upwind with her genoa despite the fact that her afterguard could see *Rainbow* was switching to a quadrilateral jib. It is an axiom of successful match racing to duplicate the sail selection of the other boat whenever you have a good lead.

When *Rainbow* tacked after rounding, *Endeavour* tacked to cover but when Vanderbilt tacked back Sopwith let him go. He realized that in a tacking duel *Rainbow* would be more efficient with her smaller jib but this is only a partial excuse. He should have covered until he saw he was losing, he should have changed jibs while still ahead, or (and this is a bit of Monday morning quarterbacking) he should have left *Rainbow* only when he felt she was on the unfavored tack. Instead, he let her go for a full forty minutes (belatedly shifting to doublehead rig), and when the weather mark was reached, *Rainbow* had a handsome lead of two minutes forty-seven seconds. On the run to the finish *Endeavour* came to life, but it was too late. She closed to within fifty-five seconds—a gallant but futile last try.

There is no question that the faster boat lost. She lost by sloppier sail handling, by a schoolboy mistake in the third race, by the inexperience of her gallant but raw, amateur crew, by less effective trimming and poorer sail selection, and in general by not playing heads up ball. As Herb Stone wrote in the October, 1934, issue of *Yachting:* "During the series it can truthfully be said that everyone made mistakes but Charles E. Nicholson —and he designed *Endeavour,* the best yacht that has ever come in quest of the America's Cup."

Three years later Sopwith sailed *Endeavour II* with consummate skill but was trounced by that super J-boat *Ranger.* Had he sailed in 1934 like he sailed in 1937, the Cup would have been his!

While the 1934 match was the biggest threat to the American's long-lasting reign, there were two other squeakers. Since I was not there I will not talk much about the 1920 match when *Resolute* so nearly lost to *Shamrock*

Endeavour *leading* Rainbow *at a start in the 1934 match.* Rainbow's *spinnaker was broken out so much faster, however, that she soon gained the lead.*

Twelves can't plane but they can surf if they catch a big sea just right. Here **Gretel** *does! The first photo shows her bow rising as a big sea sweeps by. In the second one an even bigger sea lifts her stern and in photo #3 she rides it to sweep by* **Weatherly**, *picking up several lengths in a matter of seconds. She went on to win this second race in the 1962 match by 17 seconds, the largest margin between the two boats throughout this closest race in the history of the America's Cup.*

IV, aside from reciting the bare statistics. In those days the match was a best of five series with the first boat to win three races being the winner. In the first race *Resolute* was leading comfortably when she lost her mainsail when the throat halyard parted. When her cause became hopeless she elected not to finish. No great cause for alarm since *Resolute* had been leading at the time.

Since *Shamrock* gave her approximately seven minutes time allowance *Resolute* still looked golden for the series.

The second race was something else. Despite sloppy sail handling *Shamrock* showed great speed in the light going and after being behind early swept into the lead. Thereafter she got the better of several shifts in the flukey wind and crossed ten minutes five seconds in the lead, saving her time by two minutes twenty-six seconds.

One more win and Sir Thomas Lipton's dream of winning the Cup would have been realized. In the third race the two yachts had identical elapsed times in a good sailing breeze with *Resolute* winning handily on corrected.

The series was squared in the fourth race, a flukey affair in which *Resolute* was usually in the right place at the right time to win by over three minutes on elapsed time and approximately ten minutes on corrected.

On the day scheduled for the fifth race there was a puffy twenty-three to twenty-five knot sou'wester blowing as they sailed about the starting area. Both skippers agreed with the race committee's decision to postpone. One can only wonder what would have happened if William Burton, skipper of *Shamrock IV,* had not agreed and the race had been sailed.

But it is known that on the ensuing day a fickle four knot wind was blowing. *Shamrock* got the start by forty seconds but that was her last hurrah. *Resolute* led at the windward mark of the thirty mile windward-leeward race and on the run home kept widening out to cross thirteen minutes ahead, winning by the handsome margin of nearly twenty minutes.

It had been a close series only in the fact that *Resolute* had been down by two races and one more slip would have spelled disaster. But under the conditions that prevailed for the series she proved to be the faster yacht. This coupled with better sailing gave her the wins she required when her fate was in the balance.

A still closer shave and one almost equaling *Rainbow*'s squeaker over *Endeavour* came in the 1970 series sailed in Twelve Meters. Do not be misled by the fact that *Intrepid* beat *Gretel II* four races to one. The score could have been and should have been exactly reversed! By the time the series was over most knowledgeable sailors concluded that *Intrepid* was faster in wind strengths over sixteen knots. There seemed little to choose between them in winds of twelve to fifteen except for the fact that *Gretel* accelerated faster after tacks and hence should fare better in a tacking duel. But in twelve knots and under it was all *Gretel,* not only in acceleration but in pure boat speed, especially upwind. When one then considers that only one race was sailed in a strong breeze you begin to recognize the magnitude of *Intrepid*'s achievement. In the first race there was twenty knots of wind at the start and twelve to fifteen at the finish. In race two it was six knots at the start and nine at the finish, race three ten and eighteen respectively, race four ten at the start, dropping to four to six at the finish and race five nine to ten at the start and only five at the finish—all these wind strengths being official N.Y.Y.C. recordings.

How then did skipper Bill Ficker, his tactician Steve Van Dyke, navigator Peter Wilson, and the rest of *Intrepid*'s crew do it? It is a long and fascinating story, but in essence they pulled it off by recognizing the situation early and applying unorthodox match racing tactics, aided and abetted by failure on the part of *Gretel*'s brain trust to realize soon enough just how good their boat was. They also made some pretty bad errors in judgment and revealed ignorance of a couple of key racing rules.

The first race, sailed in heavy air, was all *Intrepid.* She had an edge at the start to weather of *Gretel* and throughout the leg favored the right hand side of the course to take best advantage of a clocking wind. *Intrepid* rounded the weather mark one minute three seconds ahead, a comfortable margin but the fact that she had the better of the start and had sailed a better course also proved that *Gretel* was no pushover even in a breeze. On the first reach, although *Gretel* got a horrendous spinnaker wrap which took six minutes to unravel, she lost only five seconds. But when she lost a crew member overboard on the second reach and had to go back to recover him her goose was cooked. American supporters were lulled into complacency but on *Intrepid* they realized that *Gretel* was no slouch even in the sort of weather *Intrepid* reveled in.

The second race, started in nine knots of wind, revealed to all that *Gretel* was for real. She led at the first two marks and was close behind at the third, after which the race was abandoned due to thickening fog which made for

an unsafe situation considering the huge spectator fleet. Imagine the howls of favoritism which would have ensued if the New York Yacht Club had canceled with *Gretel* in the lead!

In the real second race *Gretel* showed her class and at the same time showed the shortcomings of her crew. In the most famous protest situation of America's Cup history she fouled at the start and got off almost dead in the water in *Intrepid*'s wake. The protest was discussed in Chapter Eight, but let it be said here that *Gretel*'s starting helmsman, Martin Visser, seemed more intent on sucking *Intrepid* into a foul than on getting a good start. He could have gotten a lovely safe leeward start. Instead, he forced a collision, and to further compound the error, he did not know the pertinent right-of-way rule and hence instead of throwing *Intrepid* out, it was *Gretel* which got the axe in the subsequent hearing.

After starting with a huge deficit, *Gretel* got going on the first beat and nearly caught *Intrepid* in a tacking duel until the latter broke it off when she was in light air letting *Gretel* tack away all by herself into a header. This enabled *Intrepid* to round the first mark 42 seconds ahead. Reaching is *Intrepid*'s strong point and this, coupled with more efficient chutes and smarter sail handling, enabled her to build her lead to 1:42 starting upwind the second time. On that beat she lost 30 seconds but still started the run with what appeared to be a safe margin.

But it was not safe for long! *Gretel* did everything right on this leg and was aided also by bringing up a fresher wind early in the leg. She slacked her backstays well off, tacked downwind at sharper angles than *Intrepid,* and ghosted into a fifty second lead at the leeward mark. There was no stopping *Gretel* now and she opened up on the last beat to a one minute seven second lead at the finish.

The score should have been one to one but even though the protest hearing quite rightly made it two to zero in *Intrepid*'s favor, Ficker and his gang knew they were in for the fight of their lives, especially if the wind stayed light. It was not too light in the third race, ten knots at the start

Most people feel that in 1970 **Gretel II** *was the fastest Twelve Meter in the world, a boat that could, and in fact should, have won the America's Cup for Australia.*

building to eighteen at the finish. Still *Intrepid* had no easy victory. Ficker forced Visser over at the start, and although he was also over, he was able to dip back first, getting away to a commanding lead. If *Gretel* had had the same initial advantage it is unlikely she could have been caught. The margins at the first four marks remained virtually constant and all under one minute. On the run to the fifth mark, *Gretel* again began closing but just as it appeared that she might actually gain the lead, *Intrepid* jibed away after being lifted and *Gretel* did not follow. Visibility was poor and Peter Wilson had calculated that their new course would take them directly to the mark. He was right and by not following, *Gretel* sailed lots of extra distance. It was blowing hard enough so that tacking down wind at the wide angle she was sailing did not increase her speed nearly enough to offset the added mileage, and she started the last beat 1:16 behind, losing only two seconds more on the last leg. Had *Gretel* gotten the start, and had she jibed at the right time, she would almost surely have won, this despite the fine sailing breeze which was close to suiting *Intrepid.*

The fourth race was *Gretel* weather yet for five legs *Intrepid* stayed ahead. She did so by getting a nice jump at the start and thereafter eschewing standard match racing tactics. Instead of applying a close cover she sailed her own race. Van Dyke and Wilson had figured the cycle of the wind phases and they kept tacking in them almost irrespective of *Gretel*. Whenever *Gretel* did not follow she lost ground. Whenever she did she gained and finally they wised up and started following. On the second reach, *Intrepid* gained by setting a ballooner instead of matching *Gretel*'s selection of a chute. *Intrepid* had lost five seconds on the preceding reach and started the third leg a scant twenty-four seconds ahead. The ballooner did its trick, however, stretching the lead to forty seconds as they started upwind the second time. Sailing pretty much her own race on the second beat and ensuing run and making no mistakes, *Intrepid* built her lead to one minute two seconds at the start of the final windward leg.

Finally the law of averages plus a bit of overconfidence caught up with

Snafus like this are one of the reasons Gretel II *lost the 1970 match to* Intrepid. *Later in this race they lost a man overboard.*

her. This was probably enough of a lead for *Intrepid* to stay ahead through careful covering. But they let *Gretel* get out on their quarter where she got a nice lift. When *Intrepid* finally tacked to cover it was too late and *Gretel* steamed by to win by 1:02, picking up over two minutes on the last leg.

With the score now three to one (remember that without the disqualification it would have been two to two) *Intrepid* was still in the driver's seat but running scared. The fifth race was the most exciting of all, and if Bill Ficker ever sailed a better race I would have to see it to believe it. I did see this one (as I had all the others) and I rate it as the best sailed race in Twelve Meter history, a race where the slower boat won despite great odds. It was nine to ten knots at the start dropping to five at the finish—*Gretel* weather! It was also a fickle northerly which provided an opportunity for tactics to offset pure boat speed.

Hardy got the start to windward of Ficker and with a one second jump. And to windward was just the place to be since there was a better breeze to the east, coupled with a tendency for the wind to haul. Ficker, Van Dyke, and Wilson suspected this and hence a few minutes after crossing the line, they tacked close under *Gretel*'s stern. If Hardy had tacked with them instead of crossing he could have kept Ficker from the favored side of the course. Once given the opening Ficker kept always a bit east of *Gretel* and despite inferior boat speed his position let him close the gap. The clincher came when *Intrepid* was approaching the mark on starboard tack and not quite fetching. It appeared that *Gretel* could cross by the narrowest of margins but instead Hardy elected to tack short in a safe leeward position. The tactic backfired when *Intrepid* got a lift a few seconds later, a lift which just enabled her to fetch while *Gretel* had to make two extra tacks just short of the mark to get around it.

Intrepid rounded forty-four seconds ahead. On the first reach she lost four seconds, on the second one she lost one more to start upwind the second time thirty-nine seconds ahead.

On the ensuing windward leg Ficker kept tacking on *Gretel* whenever he and his brain trust thought she was going the right way and then delaying her cover. Sometimes *Gretel* would tack back losing by the two extra tacks but utilizing her better speed to once again get close. Several times she

Gretel II *shown finishing ahead of* Intrepid *in the fourth race of the 1970 match. The margin isn't as close as it seems. She won by 1 minute 02 seconds, picking up more than two minutes on the last leg.*

nearly broke through, particularly late in the leg when she was on *Intrepid*'s lee bow on port tack and already on the starboard lay line for the mark. But she was so close to *Intrepid* that she could not tack and gain starboard tack rights without *Intrepid* having to alter course to avoid a collision prior to the tack's completion. Ficker kept driving Hardy ever farther past the lay line, waiting for a puff, and when it came he tacked in it and reached for the mark. Hardy waited a few seconds before following suit and by this time Ficker was riding the puff on a tight reach for the mark.

While they had been just seconds apart a few minutes before *Intrepid* had a fifty-one second lead as the run started.

She needed every bit of it. The wind had now lightened still more and both boats tacked downwind at radical angles, *Intrepid* jibing on the lifts and never letting *Gretel* get on her wind. Still *Gretel* kept coming and was less than two boat lengths and a scant twenty seconds behind at the leeward mark.

Here Ficker made his final key move. The wind had hauled to make it a near fetch to the finish on starboard tack. Instead of waiting for *Gretel* to tack before covering, he tacked immediately, figuring that this was the most direct course home and detecting what he thought was better air to the north instead of the east as in the two prior windward legs. Again he was right and built a more comfortable lead within a few minutes after rounding. Thereafter it was a question of staying always between *Gretel* and the finish yet making a few tacks as required to thus negate *Gretel*'s better ability to accelerate.

The eventual margin at the finish of one minute forty-four seconds was misleading. It was one of the closest races in Cup history, a race which Ficker would have lost if he had made a single mistake. His support boats owned by members of the syndicate had flags reading "Ficker is Quicker." Right on! Particularly in this race but also throughout most of the match it was Ficker and his crew who had prevailed over a boat which was usually going faster than *Intrepid.*

Chapter XI
When We Lose the Cup

I had originally thought of entitling this chapter, "Will We Ever Lose?" I changed it because the answer was too easy: YES. You and I may not live to see the day, or it could happen in the very next challenge, but sooner or later the American defender is going to get licked. In Chapter Ten we have seen how very close we came to losing in 1934 and 1970. There have been other matches we could have lost.

Don't get me wrong. I expect the Americans to win in 1980, and until we do lose the defender will be the favorite as each match begins. American sailors remain the best in the world but our years of dominance are not forever. A couple of decades ago who would have expected a Russian to win an Olympic gold medal in yachting? In 1960 one did in the Star Class and ever since they have been strong contenders in most Olympic classes. Russians have not competed for the America's Cup but their surge in other yachting events illustrate the increased competition we are facing. While

The America's Cup—the most coveted trophy in all of sport. Untold millions of dollars and extraordinary effort over a span of 110 years have been spent in a futile attempt to wrest it from its pedestal in the New York Yacht Club.

we usually have the best record in the yachting Olympics, there have been years that we have won no gold medals.

In ocean racing we used to be in a class by ourselves. We would send three American boats abroad to race in the famed Fastnet Race and chances were good that one of them would win, despite an entry list of over a hundred boats. Now our top boats do well but the chances of one of them winning in such a vast fleet is remote, although *Imp* did in 1977 and *Tenacious* in 1979. The Admiral's Cup, competed for by the top three ocean racers from each of nineteen different nations, has been won in recent years by teams from Australia, Germany and England, as well as by the U.S. Not too long ago an English boat won our top ocean race—The Newport-Bermuda Race.

While we are still hot, so are other nations and the number of keen contenders makes an American victory in most events a long shot. It is like basketball. It used to be a foregone conclusion that our team would win the Olympics. No longer true. Ditto in track. And who, a few years ago, would have expected a Russian hockey team to come over here and be trounced by the U.S. Olympic team?

Still, in America's Cup competition, where technology is an important part of winning, we retain an edge. Our sails, for example, are usually just a bit better, but here too the gap is closing. And in a different type of technology, it was the Australian challenger *Gretel* which was the first to have linked coffee-grinder winches.

One advantage the American boats have long enjoyed is a long series of elimination races. By the end of the summer the survivor of these races is battle-tested and honed to perfection. She used to sail against a challenger which either was the only contender, or which had at best one other boat vying for the right to challenge. And invariably they had far fewer elimination races. Now, with a number of nations challenging, and a series of elimination races comparable to our own, the lone survivor will be sharp and tough. In short, many of the built-in advantages we used to have no longer exist.

Still, as long as we keep our guard up, keep building new boats for the defense, and keep attracting our best skippers and crews we will remain very, very tough to beat. In that respect we seem to be getting tougher. In the old days skippers and crews were culled from a relative few. While they were good, often they were chosen from an inner circle and some skippers got their crack by being major financial contributors. Now every skipper and every crew member has proven his ability in tough competition. The allure of the America's Cup is such that with the exception of Buddy Melges, any skipper invited to helm a contender is quick to accept. Dennis Conner would be a leading contender for an Olympic gold medal in the Star Class but when faced with the choice of skippering either *Enterprise* or *Freedom* in the 1980 America's Cup campaign or pursuing his Olympic goals it took him little time to opt for the former. So long as sailors of his caliber are willing to go after the Cup our prospects of retaining it remain good.

This is somewhat offset, of course, by the fact that challenging nations can also ellicit their best and are going with their best as opposed to those who might come from the "right" yacht club.

Another leveller is the fact that many of the foreign designers have served apprenticeships in the U.S., most notably at Sparkman & Stephens. There are few if any secrets in how to design a competitive Twelve. The International Rule has been explored so fully that the chance of a break-through is remote, if not nonexistent. Britton Chance found this to his dismay when he tried a radical departure in 1974 and instead came up with a real turkey named *Mariner.* Minor improvements can be made. But there is no valid reason to expect them to be made by the American designers more than by the foreign ones.

A one weather match, either all heavy or all light, is apt to do us in. The Americans can be counted on to select a well-rounded defender, whereas the challenger is apt to go for an extreme design to excel in one weather condition at the expense of the other. This could well make her almost unbeatable if the conditions for which she was designed existed during the match. And the fact that either boat can ask for a lay day after each race increases the possibility (if they have a crack meteorologist) of getting the weather to their boat's liking. There is a myth to the effect that it is apt to blow hard off Newport in September. I feel that just the reverse is true and someday a fine light air Twelve is apt to lift the Cup.

When that happens it will be the end of the longest monopoly in sports history. It could also be the end of the America's Cup races as we know them. The real carrot for the challenger is the incentive to be the first to achieve the unattainable. Should we lose, the Cup competition will continue for a while as we design and build new boats and travel abroad to win it back. It is when we do win it back that I worry about the future. Will the challengers then be willing to spend the millions and exert the prodigious effort that is required to be the *second* nation to win the Cup from the Americans? Maybe so, but maybe no. Most people know that Hilary and Tensing were the first to scale Mt. Everest. But I have yet to find anyone who can name the second duo to do it. In fact, most people don't even realize it has been scaled many times, including more difficult routes to the summit.

Many people know also that Roger Bannister was the first man to run a mile in less than four minutes but it takes a real track afficionado to name the current world record holder despite the fact that his time would have put him 70 or 80 yards ahead of Bannister's best effort. And let's not kid ourselves. The great publicity the America's Cup enjoys is a big reason for competing for it. And publicity could wane after we have lost.

It is well for Americans who feel that it would be "good for the sport" (and there are many of them) if we lost the America's Cup to ruminate on these thoughts. The America's Cup races are unique for many reasons, but most of all because they represent the longest unbeaten string in any sport. Keeping it so is the surest way to maintain and increase its appeal. With the way sailing is developing around the world we need every American rooting for us to keep this unique "Mt. Everest" inviolate and growing in stature the longer it remains unscaled.

Chapter XII
Sailing for the America's Cup

0930, September 15, 1964—The dock at Newport Shipyard was jammed with shipyard workers, syndicate members, crew wives, girl friends, and anyone else who could scrounge a pass to what was at that moment the most exclusive piece of waterfront in Newport, Rhode Island. As I kissed Charlotte goodby, she said with calm conviction, "You can do it, Bob." I waved to my oldest son Rob, my daughters Louise and Anne, hopped aboard *Constellation* as the dock lines from *Chaperone* were cast off precisely at 0930. We had developed the habit of leaving at the exact moment we had decided we would leave, not a minute earlier or later, and the fact that we were on our way to tow out for the first race of the 18th match for the America's Cup made it seem even more vital to be punctual.

As the last line was cast off and our tender *Chaperone* surged ahead, with *Constellation* nestled alongside her, the crowd ashore shouted, whistled, waved, clapped, blew kisses (the females that is) and exhorted us into battle with the usual inanities. From the yachts still at the pier, and from a swarm of others milling around just off it, air horns and deep throated ship's whistles raised a discordant and deafening chorus. Just as our stern cleared the dock, the cannon manned by the shipyard workers thundered their own special salute. Their's was the most fervent exhortation because to a man they had bet up to a month's wages on *Constellation,* often at big odds or even money for a clean sweep. It crossed my mind that if we did not win it might be aimed at us, and loaded with more than blanks upon our return.

Once clear of the dock we cast off the bow, stern and spring lines from *Chaperone* while she surged ahead with the towing line sucking out astern of her. As Rod Stephens put our large American ensign in our stern socket, I was swept with an inexplicable shortness of breath. "For God's sakes, Bob, don't be so corny," I muttered to myself but to no avail.

From the Williams & Manchester dock we saw *Sovereign* getting underway and now it was their turn to receive an equally loud send-off. "Well, we're ahead of them already," someone remarked, and everyone laughed as though they had just heard the best joke of their lives.

As we passed Fort Adams, towing now at nine knots, the throngs ashore waved like madmen. I perceived one family holding what looked like a bedsheet with a message written on it. I grabbed the binoculars, and was really moved to read the words, "Good luck, *Connie.*" I did not know who they were but I have wished ever since that I could tell them how much I appreciated that message, referring to *Constellation* by the nickname we so often used for her.

As we passed Castle Hill, the entire staff of our summer home was on the lawn waving towels as though they were shipwrecked sailors trying to attract the first ship they had seen in months. One of them dipped the American flag, another manned their signal cannon, firing in rapid sequence.

Then we were clear of the land, but surrounded by a vast armada of spectator craft with hundreds more following us out from Newport and small planes and a Goodyear blimp overhead. Everyone seemed overcome with America's Cup fever and for us eleven, it was a sendoff unlike others in a lifetime of sailing. We loved it and appreciated it. Instead of building my confidence it merely emphasized the importance of not blowing it, not letting these thousands of well wishers down by sailing poorly.

Now the hard part. It was an hour's tow to the starting area with absolutely nothing to do. The sails had been selected, the weather checked. *Constellation* was as ready as a boat can be. Often I took a snooze on the tow out, but on this day I wanted to savor the excitement from watching the armada going out to watch us. It was heartwarming and exciting, but did nothing to still the butterflies which were doing a war dance in my stomach. "It's just another race," I told myself, but of course it wasn't. I did convince myself, however, that in all probability, *Sovereign* would be easier than *American Eagle,* but we couldn't be sure. And it was the America's Cup that was on the line.

0900, August 31, 1974—For some inexplicable reason I was feeling pretty good as I walked down the dock at Newport Shipyard to board *Courageous* for what could be the last race of the final trials to select the defender. I had little reason to be happy. After winning four straight races against *Intrepid* I had managed to lose three straight, and we now stood all even in the final trials at four wins apiece. In one of our losses, we were slightly ahead of *Intrepid* but elected not to cover because we expected a header which would give us a safe lead. When instead we got a lift it cooked our goose, and that evening I had to be polite when one of the crew wives started educating me on the importance of covering in a match race. And just the day before, in a race which was called because of an impending storm, I had blown a lead by setting a floater spinnaker on the reach instead of a three-quarter ounce tri-radial. That evening another wife asked me why I had just let *Intrepid* reach by without luffing her. She did not seem very convinced when I pointed out that it is suicide to luff with a floater against a boat with a reaching chute.

If the wives were concluding that Bob Bavier was pretty dumb, I was sure that the crew must be of the same persuasion.

Perhaps I was feeling better on this particular morning because I felt things could not get worse and hence might well get better. But there was another reason. The previous evening I had what I considered to be a good discussion with Ted Hood and Halsey Herreshoff. I pointed out that we had lost our lead the previous day by deferring too much to each other and having too many cooks, which had slowed our decision making.

It was decided that after Dennis Connor started and Ted Hood took over as helmsman on the windward leg, I would make the final decision on upwind tactics, with Halsey and Dennis giving me their thinking but only me advising Ted. Then when we rounded the windward mark, and I started steering, Ted was to concentrate on sail trim and sail selection, including when a spinnaker should be replaced. Halsey was to be the key tactician on the leeward legs, getting input from Dennis and Ted, but he alone communicating their thoughts to me. Earlier, I had made the mistake of not making it clear who was primarily responsible for what, with the end result that there was either too much talking or too little fast decision making. By clearing up the priorities and responsibilities, I felt we would operate more smoothly and decisively. Ted and Halsey seemed to agree.

Thus buoyed up, and encouraged also by the conviction that *Courageous* was now a slight bit faster than *Intrepid,* I felt surprisingly confident as I strode down the dock. Half way to *Courageous* was the imposing figure of Bob McCullough, head of our syndicate. He was all alone and apparently waiting for me. He didn't look happy. As I drew near, he stepped forward to meet me and with only a perfunctory "Good morning, Bob" instead of his customary hearty greeting, he then blurted out the fateful words—"The syndicate has had a meeting and we feel you should get off the boat." Those might not have been the exact words but they were close.

Suddenly it wasn't such a sparkling day. For a moment I thought that this might be the opening gambit of a discussion, rather than a decision. "Have you talked to Halsey?" I asked.

"Yes."

"How's he feel about it?" I asked.

"He approves."

"How about Ted?"

"Yes, he knows and is ready to take over, and some of the crew know too, and they are in favor."

All of a sudden, it was apparent that this was not a discussion Bob and I were having. It was an irrevocable decision.

163

Just at this time, Charlotte came down the dock to board *Escort* to watch the race. She took one look at Bob and me and with her usual good sense kept right on walking past us.

If I had still had any questions about whether or not a firm decision had been made, it was dispelled when Bob showed me a neatly typed press release. It commenced with the statement that Bob and I had been friends since we were kids, and that the previous evening we had had a long discussion about what was best for *Courageous,* and I had volunteered to get off and turn her over to Ted Hood. It had some other statements which made me look good. The rub was that aside from the statement of our being longtime friends (we still are) there was not a shred of truth to it. All of a sudden I wished there had been, but I simply had not become convinced that I couldn't pull it off. What's that saying about an athlete being the last to recognize that he has slipped a bit, lost that extra step? "OK, Bob, I'll go along with your decision," (as if I had a choice), "but that press release has to go. When they ask me, I'll tell them I was kicked off."

We left it at that and as Bob went to give the word to the crew, I gave Charlotte the bad word. She wasn't as surprised as I had been but she did her best to make me feel better. She was surprised, however, at the timing and she did not like the press release any more than I. "What are you going to do now?" she asked.

"Break in on the meeting Bob is having with the crew, wish them well and tell Ted and the others that I know they can pull it off. Then I'm going out on *Escort* and watch the race."

I not only went out and watched, but spent most of the time steering *Escort,* as if to prove to myself, if no one else, that at least I could handle a powerboat. To make things harder the wind never came up enough to permit a start, which allowed more than the usual time for everyone to see me in an unusual place. It was almost funny (though I did not think so at the time) to see the startled looks on the faces of friends, the press and spectators when they recognized me on *Escort*'s flying bridge instead of on *Courageous.* They did not seem to know whether to wave, or look away or whether or not to say anything. It wasn't easy to take, but was nothing compared to the look on the faces of my daughters, Louise and Anne, who had already embarked on a friend's boat to see their Dad take on *Intrepid* in what could be the last race of the summer.

1224, September 15, 1964—After the long tow out to the America's Cup buoy we had a further delay because the Coast Guard had trouble clearing the vast spectator fleet from the starting area.

Finally, at 1215, course signals were hoisted. In 20 minutes the start would be history. We had decided to be aggressive at the first start even though we felt *Constellation* was faster than *Sovereign.* First of all, you could not be sure. Secondly, it seemed important to convince Peter Scott at the outset that he couldn't push us around, and that we enjoyed aggressive starts. If we proved faster, he would not be encouraged to be overly aggressive in subsequent starts. But most important was the matter of pride. With thousands of my peers watching, I wanted to prove I could get a good start.

With eleven minutes to go we were approaching *Sovereign,* reaching on a reciprocal course, us to leeward. "This time we hook up," I told the crew, "but make it look as though we won't." Now with something immediate to think about, something to do, the butterflies in my stomach went away. Or perhaps I was too busy concentrating to notice them.

As we neared *Sovereign* our crew was lounging on deck as if they were out for a Sunday sail. I tried to look casual too, looking at *Sovereign* only out of the corner of my eye. But just after we passed bow to bow I spun to windward, the crew lept to their feet and trimmed furiously and before Peter knew what had happened and could bear off we were squarely on *Sovereign*'s tail. We had her where we wanted her. The question was, could we keep her there? As *Sovereign* jibed, tacked and jibed again we maintained our position just one length astern. I was pleased to note we could turn even sharper and maintain speed. There were a couple of instants when we might have turned inside of her, or held our starboard tack, and perhaps hit her when she jibed to port. But the last thing we wanted was to win the first start by inducing a foul. We were content to follow like a dog on heel, knowing this position gave us the option of breaking off the circle at the time we thought best for us.

With two-and-a-half minutes to go and several lengths below the line, Peter jibed, then trimmed and headed toward the line to make still one more

Favorite breakfast pastime was reading what the press had to say about yesterday's race. This is Constellation's *crew at Castle Hill in 1964.*

circle. We elected not to follow but instead reached off to leeward and then, with a minute-and-a-half remaining, tacked for the line, tight reaching for a spot a couple of lengths to leeward of the Committee boat, the end we preferred. This would enable us to hit the line with full headway, while *Sovereign,* being so close to the line and having to make an extra circle, would surely be going slower. But we could still lose the start if not timed perfectly. And we had to be wary of barging.

Peter played it perfectly, tacking on our bow to assume a safe leeward position. With our extra speed we could break through to leeward, provided we had it timed just right. But I preferred to go past to windward.

The trouble with that was the proximity of the Committee boat. Peter could luff until the gun fired and, if he did, we could be squeezed out.

"Better drive through to leeward," I said to myself and shouted, "Trim for speed!" as I bore off a few degrees. Peter was watching and bore off with us, smack on our wind. But we were going nine and one half knots, at least three knots faster than *Sovereign,* and it looked like we could drive on through into a safe leeward.

Then a better opportunity dawned on me. As *Sovereign* bore off, the gap widened between her and the Committee boat. No longer was there any danger of being squeezed out. The trouble is that when I said "trim for speed" and bore off everyone aboard surmised we were committed to going through to leeward. The bow man, Buddy Bombard, stopped calling distance between our bow and *Sovereign*'s stern, quite rightly calling only distance from the line.

There was no time for discussion or for asking whether we could swing her stern. Instead, if I wanted to go by to windward, I had to chance it and swing up without a second's delay. A summer of sailing in close quarters gives you a pretty close eye. I knew our bow was not overlapped, but we were closing so much faster that it was going to be mighty close by the time we swung up.

I spun the wheel, said a silent prayer and as I did, our great crew trimmed for the new unexpected course without a word being spoken. There simply was not time to say anything. Buddy told me later that we cleared by twelve feet, close enough since we were going three knots faster.

As the gun went off, our bow was thirty feet in front and we were a full length to windward. Rod and Eric cheered in unison.

My mouth was suddenly very dry and I asked for a stick of gum. A few minutes later when we were several lengths ahead of *Sovereign* and right on her wind when she made her first tack I relaxed and thought to myself, "This racing for the America's Cup is fun."

1800, September 3, 1974—There were tears running down several of the faces of *Intrepid*'s crew. Others seemed to be having trouble swallowing. Skipper Gerry Driscoll was dry-eyed and had a tight smile on his face as he led the way onto the Newport Shipyard dock to congratulate Ted Hood

The hardest job of the America's Cup Committee is notifying the loser that they are eliminated. In 1974 it was particularly hard to tell Intrepid *that she was out. Skipper Gerry Driscoll (kneeling) keeps up a brave front but the rest of his crew is close to tears.*

and the crew of *Courageous.* Two hours before, *Courageous* had beaten *Intrepid* by a minute and a half in a heavy air race—the very wind that the press had kept referring to all summer as *"Intrepid* weather." The Selection Committee had paid their respective visits, first giving *Intrepid* the bad news, then notifying *Courageous* that she was to defend the Cup, having won five, lost four to *Intrepid* in the final trials.

We had been whooping it up on *Courageous,* but a sudden hush fell as

168

All hail the conquering heroes as Courageous *heads home after beating* Southern Cross *4–0 in 1974.*

Intrepid's crew arrived. They said kind words, and were congratulated in turn for putting up such a magnificent fight in an "old" 1967 wooden boat. Everyone had a swig or two of champagne, and smiles broke out all around. But half of the bunch was dying inside and the other half was acting embarassed, knowing the pain their summer-long rivals were feeling.

Perhaps I could best read their thoughts. I had had my own disappointment a few days before, being kicked off as skipper, and the hurt still

It wasn't long after Courageous's *final victory in 1974 before her entire crew as well as innocent bystanders were heaved overboard.*

lingered. A yachting reporter friend of mine whispered to me, "This America's Cup racing is a damned meat grinder, a destroyer of men." "I know what you mean," I replied.

Intrepid's crew did not linger long. When they left, and even later back at Hammersmith Farm for our victory dinner, the celebrating was strangely subdued for a crew just notified that they had been selected to defend the America's Cup.

1810, August 30, 1977—I donned my traditional cocoanut hat, bedecked with the New York Yacht Club ribbon and joined the rest of the Selection Committee as we boarded our tender to pay the fateful call on *Enterprise.* *Courageous* had just beaten her by a minute twenty-six seconds, her sixth straight victory over her arch rival in the final trials. A thunderstorm was approaching, but we did not want to delay longer. We had seen enough. A few days earlier, Lowell North had been replaced by Mahlin Burnham as skipper of *Enterprise,* but to no avail. All it did, said Ted Turner to me as we got the word during a cocktail party, was add a distinguished new member to our "club"—the group of sailors who had been relieved as America's Cup skippers. Lowell had twice won the Star Worlds and was an Olympic gold medalist. "Our club's getting real class," exulted Ted.

As we approached the Williams & Manchester dock we could see the sudden turning of heads by the *Enterprise* crew and could almost lip read their remarks—"My God, they're coming." Mahlin seemed particularly stunned. He had lost by close margins in the races he sailed and in the last one had gained forty-two seconds on the last leg. Obviously he had not expected the axe so soon and in fact we interrupted them in the process of checking delivery of a new sail due the next day. The loser always feels the elimination series had been too short and, despite *Courageous'* superb record, they had not given up hope. Once over their initial surprise, however, they took it well. It was not the emotional blockbuster of three years before when *Intrepid* was dismissed.

As soon as we arrived the storm hit, accompanied by torrential rain. We huddled inside *Enterprise*'s tender, fast running out of things to say and wishing the rain would quit. Finally it did and we scampered back aboard our tender and powered over to Newport Shipyard. Ted Turner and his crew were expecting us. They had watched us out of the corner of their eyes as we headed toward *Enterprise* and were lined up Navy-style as we came alongside *Courageous.* Just as we got there and just as George Hinman blurted the traditional words, "Captain Turner, I have the honor to inform you and the crew of *Courageous* that you have been selected to defend the America's Cup," the sun broke through. Talk about symbolism!

It was a happy visit, enlivened by champagne which appeared on cue from the bilge of *Courageous.* It remained happy and little strained upon the arrival of the *Enterprise* crew, despite the flow of nasty words which had been exchanged by the two camps throughout the summer. The real shock only comes in a cliff-hanger elimination.

Seeing the exuberant faces on board, made me reminisce on the excitement I had felt thirteen years earlier—the first time I had started against *American Eagle* and the first time we had beaten her, the race in the final trials when we trailed at all five marks only to sweep by a mile from the finish —a win which gave us the confidence to know we would eventually gain selection, and then finally the thrill of competing for the Cup itself against *Sovereign.* Lowell North joined the group and this made me think of other things, despite Lowell's brave front. We did not stay long. It was a joyous occasion but we knew full well that this crew would have even more fun when we left.

1600, September 21, 1964—A strange thing was happening. We had beaten *Sovereign* decisively in the first three races of the nineteenth match for the America's Cup and now on the last leg of the fourth race we had an absolutely unbeatable lead. We had rounded the last mark with a lead of twelve minutes twenty-six seconds, a margin of nearly two miles. The wind was steady, yet gentle enough so that a breakdown (the only possible way of being caught) was out of the question. We were staying between *Sovereign* and the finish, making a loose cover and we were opening up distance with every passing minute. If ever there were the ingredients for a "yawner" they were here. But the strange part was that I could feel a growing excitement among our crew. The jib snapped home after every tack with the precision of a quarterback making a hand-off to his fullback. I was steering with as much intensity as if *Sovereign* were one length astern and gaining. We had decided long ago, as soon as we determined that *Constellation* was faster, that no matter how far ahead we got we would never hold back in order to make the race look more respectable. We knew that if Peter Scott knew we were holding back he would not like it. Many times in the series we rooted for *Sovereign* to make it closer after we had a commanding lead. We agonized when we saw her make a desperation tack or jibe which we knew full well would put her even further behind. But while we really

Peter Scott never won a race against Constellation *but such was his charm that he never lost a press conference. Left to right: Peter, moderator Bus Mosbacher, me and Eric Ridder.*

wished she would do better we never had any part in making her look better, always trying to sail *Constellation* to her utmost. Still, some of the races, after the first mile or two, were pretty dull, not only for the spectator fleet but for us as well.

Why then the excitement we all felt on this last leg of what would surely be the last race in the nineteenth match for the America's Cup? Finally it dawned on me that we had all contacted "America's Cup fever." No other sailing event could engender such excitement when the outcome was so obvious. But this was not just some other sailing event. This was the America's Cup, and we were about to win it and we suddenly wanted to win it in style.

Constellation foamed ahead, slicing through the seas left over from the previous day's fresh breeze. Many of us would never sail on her again or

Constellation *is roaring for the line and* Sovereign *tacks ahead of her in hopes of blanketing or gaining a safe leeward.*

When Sovereign *also bears off there is room to pass to windward and, in a last second change of plan, I swing* Constellation *across her stern, clearing* Sovereign *by just a few feet.*

We on Constellation *are fearful of barging (the Committee boat is just out of the picture to the right) and hence bear off to pass to leeward.*

Constellation's *greater headway approaching the line allows us to gain this lovely position as the gun goes. Our bow is a half-length ahead, we have greater headway and are hard on the wind while* Sovereign *is forced to bear off to gain speed and keep her wind clear.*

The telephoto lens is deceiving. Constellation *is already two minutes ahead of* Sovereign *on the second leg of the first race in 1964.*

on any boat so deserving of being called a thoroughbred. We wanted to do her proud. And we did. We picked up more than three minutes on that last leg alone to win by fifteen minutes, thirty seconds.

And when we crossed the line, and heard the gun, both Rod and I

As Constellation *crosses the line in the last race of the 1964 match Rod and I instinctively give her a pat for a job well done.*

instinctively and simultaneously patted *Constellation*'s topsides for a job well done, while the crew erupted with the enthusiasm one would expect from a come-behind victory of less than a length.

Sailing for the America's Cup can mean different things to different people. It can tear your heart out. It can bring strong men to the brink of a nervous breakdown and can leave scars which while diminishing through the years, will ever remain like a surgeon's most skilled incision. For persistent challengers like Thomas Lipton and Baron Bich it can become an obsession, the more virulent, the longer the quest goes unfulfilled. But for the fortunate few who have tasted victory, who have enjoyed the comradeship

Only an America's Cup victory could engender such enthusiasm as we all felt on Constellation *after routing* Sovereign *by a huge margin in the final race of 1964.*

of a summer with an extraordinary group of teammates, and who have had the privilege of doing battle with other groups of extraordinary men, it becomes, for a while at least, the most important thing in life. Once it is all over, and you drift back into the main stream of life, either licking your wounds or exulting for ever more in the greatest victory a sailor can have, you come to realize that America's Cup fever is nothing to laugh about. Once stricken, you won't ever get over it completely. But win or lose it is an unforgettable experience, and either way you might be the better for it.

Chapter XIII
Challenge 1980

There's always an air of expectancy and uncertainty in each America's Cup year. Even when the challenge appears to pose no great threat one can never be sure that this is not going to be the year the Cup goes overseas. In 1970, for example, we appeared to be on particularly strong ground with three new boats building for defense (*Valiant* by S&S, *Heritage* by Morgan and *Intrepid,* so redesigned by Chance as to be virtually new), yet that was the very year we came so very close to losing to *Gretel II.*

In 1980 a number of factors indicate that the Americans are facing the sternest challenge in the history of the Cup. First of all, there are more challengers with *Australia* and *Sverige,* returning to be joined by two new boats, *France III* and *Lionheart.* There is also a possibility that *Gretel II* will return for still another go.

More important than the number of challengers is the fact that they have scheduled a series of elimination races comparable to our own so that the winner of their trials will be just as battle-tested as the defender. Important, too, is the fact that even the two new boats *France III* and *Lionheart* were completed in early 1979 and spent that summer shaking down both boat and crew. There's never before been such preparation, never before such a determined effort to lift the Cup.

This is being written at the end of 1979, but even as of that date I was able to learn a great deal about the various boats, both challengers and defenders. Here's the picture as I view it.

The Challengers

The challengers are being presented in alphabetical order partly for convenience, partly because I do not know for sure which one poses the most serious threat. But I do have some intuitive feelings which will become evident as we assess each boat and crew.

One thing I am confident of—there isn't a dog in the lot. In a few prior matches there have been some pretty slow challengers but the International Rule is now so fully explored that there is no longer any secret as to how to design a fast Twelve.

Australia

The 1977 challenger will be back. In reporting on that match for *Yachting* magazine I expressed the view that if crews and jibs had been swapped *Australia* would have won. If she wasn't as fast as *Courageous* she was very nearly so. Her headsails were inferior and she wasn't sailed as well. Even so, she made it close.

The 1977 challenger Australia *remains the boat to beat in 1980. She came closer to winning in 1977 than most people realized and a new rig, new sails and minor hull refinements should make her tougher in 1980.*

Since then *Australia* has been somewhat modified, nothing drastic but perhaps enough to make for a meaningful improvement. The biggest modification is a new mast. The one she used in 1977 was not sufficiently stiff and the new one could be of tremendous help in making the jib set better.

Australia's rudder, keel and after part of her underbody have all been given minor changes. In 1977 she was hard to steer but now stays very nicely in the groove.

Alan Bond is behind the 1980 challenge as he was in 1977 and 1974. The past experience is bound to help in the same vein that the '77 campaign was far better run than the earlier one. At this writing it has not been decided whether Noel Robbins will return as skipper. Another possibility is Ben Lexcen (Bob Miller), as good a sailor as he is a designer. In any event, there is no dearth of sailing talent down under and *Australia* will be well sailed. In December, *Australia* and *Gretel* will engage in a series of races. *Australia* is expected to win and the series is intended more for sharpening up her crew than anything else. Look for the selection of skipper to be announced shortly thereafter.

Based on her proven speed and the fact that she has surely been improved, *Australia* will be the boat to beat as the foreign trials begin.

France III

In three different campaigns backed by Baron Marcel Bich the French have yet to win a single race against other challengers. They have come close, have led at several marks but have always managed to find a way to lose.

This time it could well be different. In *France III,* Johan Valentijn has quite obviously come up with a fast boat. She was completed in the spring of 1979 and spent that summer in Newport racing against *Intrepid.* At summer's end, *France* had slightly the better record. *Intrepid* was not quite up to

France III, *with her tri-color topsides, is more than a striking boat. At long last Baron Bich has a formidable contender.*

fighting trim since her sails were a bit tired but Gerry Driscoll was sailing her which makes *France*'s victories all the more meaningful.

To go all the way *France III* has to be improved still further. This is already underway. In 1979 she sailed with an articulated keel and rudder and this has now been scrapped. The more conventional approach should help.

An extreme effort will be made on her sails. They were just fair in 1979 but the fact she did as well as she did with rather poor sails shows how inherently fast she is.

Bruno Troublé, who is *France III*'s skipper, has fine credentials. He served as crew on the French Soling in the 1976 Olympics (they won two races) and since then has won the European Soling Championship as skipper. He has also done a good deal of ocean racing and ranks now as one of the top sailors in France.

One cross Troublé has to bear is sharing the helm with Baron Bich. Troublé takes the start and then reverts to tactician as the Baron steers upwind. Downwind Troublé takes over as both helmsman and tactician. The Baron has retired as head of his hugely successful business and spends most of his time on the Cup campaign, with many hours on the wheel. He has become a good Twelve Meter helmsman and since Troublé will be calling the shots the system might work, though most sailors feel there must be a better windward helmsman in the country.

It is, however, the Baron's money, he has developed his skills and he is getting a great kick out of racing *France III.* The whole campaign is being run as a business. The crew, though ostensibly not professionals, spends so much time on the effort that they have to be receiving financial aid.

In the winter of 1980 Troublé, the Baron and a number of key crew members will be match racing a pair of Six Meters in California, culminating in Troublé competing in the Congressional Cup. They have felt weak in the tactics of match racing and this may cure that deficiency.

If determination, desire and long range planning will produce a winner, *France III* is a serious threat. If her sails can be improved she will be very hard to beat, because she has proven already to be a top-flight Twelve. At the very least she should win some races in 1980 and she has a chance to go all the way.

Gretel II

It is unlikely that *Gretel II* will be back but she must be included since the Aussies have left the door open. *Australia* has been beating her in recent races down under and *Gretel II*'s prospects are extremely dim. She is a fine Twelve, almost as fast as the newer boats but a pretty sure way to lose in a match race is to be almost as fast. If *Gretel* does come it will be to enable the group which is contemplating a 1983 challenge in a new boat to learn from the experience. She has to be the long shot of all potential challengers.

Lionheart

After a gap of 16 years the British are coming back and this time they are for real. *Lionheart* is designed by Ian Howlett, a bright young designer, and in his first Twelve Meter he has come up with a good one. She has been sailing since the spring of 1979 and from the very outset has been impressive. I can remember the early reports on the two previous British challengers, *Sceptre* in 1958 and *Sovereign* in 1964. Both had trouble beating Twelves which were known to be over the hill. Not so *Lionheart*. She has not only beaten older Twelves like *Constellation* which is still surprisingly slippery but she has annihilated both *Gretel II* and *Sverige*. Remember that *Sverige* was runner up to *Australia* among the 1977 challengers. *Lionheart* has beaten her more decisively, though this shouldn't be given undue significance because *Sverige* has not been campaigned agressively. Still it is most encouraging for the British. *Lionheart* is particularly impressive in light air but she won in heavy air too.

Last November I had lunch with Tony Boyden, *Lionheart*'s principal backer. In light of his boat's record I was surprised to find him not very optimistic. He realizes that it wasn't *Australia* or the new American Twelves he was beating. He felt his boat was good but considered the sails mediocre at best. He even went so far as to question if he would bother to send *Lionheart* to America unless her sails could be improved drastically. Obviously he is still hurting from *Sovereign*'s embarrassing loss to *Constellation* in

1964 and doesn't want history to repeat. He need have no such fears because this time he has a far better boat. She might well lose but not by such huge margins.

Actually his concern makes me give *Lionheart* a better chance than if he was exuding confidence. It's a form of realism which the British have sometimes lacked in the past. Being aware of the problem he has with sails will insure an all-out effort to improve them and I cannot really conceive of this promising new boat not showing up.

Lionheart's skipper John Oakeley has the finest credentials. He has excelled in Tempests, Flying Dutchmen and a variety of other classes. He has fierce dedication to go along with his natural ability and the combination is apt to get the most out of his boat. He wrote a fine book on yacht racing entitled *Winning*. He does not subscribe to the old British philosophy that "it matters not whether you win or lose—it's how you play the game." John Oakeley feels there's only one basic reason to race and that is to win and no effort is too great to achieve that goal.

Being a thoroughly nice guy he will get enough fun from the effort to stay loose and to bear up under the pressures of an America's Cup campaign. I expect *Lionheart* not only to show up but also to make her presence very much felt. If her sails do improve she could become the challenger and this year's challenger has a real chance to go all the way.

Sverige

Sverige, after *Gretel II,* has to be considered the dark horse of 1980. She barely beat *Gretel II* last time and she was no match for *Australia.* Now with two promising new boats to cope with she has her hands full.

Her skipper Pelle Peterson, however, is as good as they come. For years he has been a world class skipper in the formidable Star class. He designed *Sverige* and proof of his desiging ability is the fact that he also designed and skippered the 1979 Six Meter World Cup champion *Irene* against the largest

The British are back and in Lionheart *they have more than just a brave name. She had a superb record in her maiden year of 1979.*

187

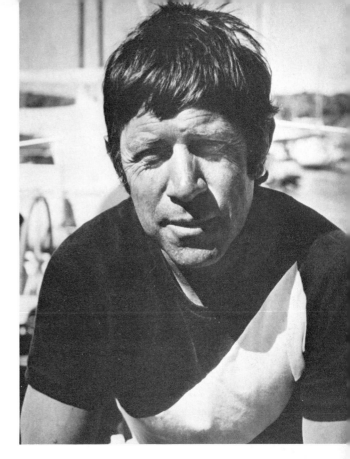

Pelle Peterson, skipper of Sverige *in 1977 and again in 1980. He is a superb sailor and like Ted Hood also an accomplished designer and sailmaker. Still, he ranks as a dark horse.*

(25) and finest group of Sixes ever assembled. The experience of a prior America's Cup campaign should help him.

The unknown factor is how well set up *Sverige* was in 1979. Unknown too are the changes to be made to her in the winter of 1980. If Pelle can adapt some of the go-fast characteristics he put into his new Six Meter (which, don't forget, was designed to the same International Rule as the Twelves), she could prove a surprise. He is a realist and is not the type to go to the effort of another America's Cup campaign unless he is holding better cards than are apparent at the moment. While I do consider her a dark horse she must be given a chance.

Sverige *is not a bad Twelve but she must be improved before being rated more than a dark horse in 1980.*

The Defenders

In the face of such a formidable challenge, it is fortunate that the Americans have a superb group of boats which will be vying for the role of defender. There are two very good veterans of prior campaigns and two new ones with great credentials. In my mind there has never before been such a fine group of defense candidates, just as there has never before been such an array of talented challengers. Both sets of elimination trials should be a real battle royal, leading up to what could well be the most exciting match. As in the case of the challengers, the defenders will be discussed in alphabetical order.

Courageous

The 1974 and 1977 defender will be back. Not only will Ted Turner skipper her, as he did in the last defense, but her entire crew will be back with him. True they will be three years older but sailing isn't like other sports where youth is so important. They were the best crew last time and their experience together should make them even better in 1980. It will be very difficult to outsail them. To win the other boats have to not only be sailed extremely well—they will probably have to be a shade faster.

We talked a lot about Ted Turner in the chapter on America's Cup skippers and hence there is no need to go further than to note that he appears to be sailing even better. The year of the last defense he won the Congressional Cup. In 1979 he amassed an outstanding record with his ocean racer, *Tenacious,* including first in the gale-swept Fastnet Race. He sails incessantly, both big boats and small, and he sails them well. I detect in him an increase in confidence and along with it a greater maturity of judgement. He will not beat himself, nor will his crew. It will take a better skipper and crew or a fine skipper and crew in a better boat to beat *Courageous.* Another thing Turner and his crew have going for them—they've been there before and there is no chance of them choking. Instead they will, as in the past have fun, sail loose, albeit intensely, and get the most out of their considerable ability.

Courageous, sporting her new snubbed bow and sliced transom. She is otherwise pretty much the same. Turner and his entire crew of 1977 will be back, giving their all to make her the first three-time defender.

The fact that *Courageous* is now six years old is a bit of a handicap. Not that she is going any slower, but in the years since she was launched designers have had an opportunity to improve on her. *Courageous* has been modified in a minor way. Her bow has been snubbed and her transom now has a more pronounced reverse slope, thus saving a bit of weight where weight reduction is so vitally important. Under water she is little changed —just the barest of refinement. The fact that the International Rule and all its ramifications have been so thoroughly explored through the years makes it very difficult to make big improvements. A true breakthrough design is impossible but it is not at all impossible to make modest improvements. In fact, I am confident that fast as she is, *Courageous* is no longer the fastest Twelve. It is this fact which will be the biggest obstacle in her way to becoming the first three time defender of the America's Cup.

Enterprise and Freedom

These two fine Twelves are lumped together because they are in the same camp and only one of them will compete in the defender trials. It is altogether possible that they are the two fastest Twelves in the world and it seems almost incomprehensible that one of them will become a trial horse instead of a true contender. But when the syndicate supporting these two boats asked Dennis Conner to be their skipper he agreed but only on the basis that he could choose which of the two boats he wanted and the other one would then become only a trial horse and not enter the elimination races. I do not know anyone other than Dennis who likes this arrangement. The New York Yacht Club does not, yachtsmen do not and all who are interested in keeping the Cup do not. Dennis justifies the arrangement on the basis that having a hot trial horse will be the surest way to hone to perfection the boat he elects to sail. I buy this up to a point. *Enterprise* and *Freedom* brushed with each other throughout the summer of 1979. In the fall both were shipped to California and will continue brushing, will continue sail testing. Since the sails are interchangeable there is no better way to determine which ones are faster. But once the trials get underway the most effective way to stimulate the boat Conner has selected would be, I feel, to have the discard racing against her. Apparently, there is no chance of this

Freedom *(to windward)* and Enterprise *could be the two fastest defense candidates, yet one is destined to become just a trial horse. Only Dennis Conner likes this agreement.*

happening but on this sort of thing one can never be certain. In between the different series of trials there would be some value in having a trial horse but couldn't this have been accomplished by having the other boat as a friendly enemy with an agreement reached to work with each other between races?

In 1977 most people expected *Enterprise* to prove faster than *Courageous.* She was created by the same design firm, Sparkman & Stephens, and had the benefit of exhaustive tank testing. The tank showed her to be an improvement, yet on the race course *Courageous* took charge. I feel this was for two basic reasons. First, Ted Turner and his crew got more out of *Courageous* both as regards to boat speed and also match race tactics. Secondly, *Enterprise* had a much smaller base to her foretriangle—a full three feet less. Wind tunnel tests had indicated this would be faster but it didn't work out that way. Not only did it require *Enterprise* to use a shorter spinnaker pole which hurt her downwind but also it hurt her acceleration after tacks. *Enterprise* was fast when she settled down on a long tack but she fared poorly in tacking duels. And in match racing ability to tack well is the name of the game.

When *Freedom* and *Enterprise* started brushing with each other in 1979, *Enterprise* first had her original narrow foretriangle. The new boat quickly demonstrated her superiority, especially in tacking. Then *Enterprise* had her foretriangle base enlarged to match that of *Freedom.* The improvement was noticeable. There is now considerable evidence to support the contention that if *Enterprise* had had this same foretriangle in 1977 she would have been faster than *Courageous.* She certainly is now faster than she was three years ago, largely because of her larger jibs, but partly because of minor refinements. In any event she is unquestionably a very fine Twelve Meter.

What about *Freedom?* She did not undergo tank testing but does reflect her designer's thinking as to the latest state of the art in Twelve Meter design. The most obvious difference is lower freeboard, a la *Australia.* In other respects she is a refinement as opposed to a break with the past.

In October of 1979 I spent a day watching *Enterprise* and *Freedom* sail against each other. These were not races but instead speed tests with sails being interchanged between tests. At first I was on the tender and I noticed that *Freedom* made a bit less fuss going through the water. She pitched a bit less and stayed in the groove better. I spent the last few hours of the day on board *Enterprise,* with Dennis Conner sailing her. Throughout the day *Freedom* had the edge. She pointed higher and footed at least as well. With certain sails she barely edged *Enterprise,* with others she was far superior. But the important point was that at all times and no matter which sails she was using, *Freedom* was the faster boat. She also seemed to be a shade faster downwind when we set chutes to return to port at the end of the day.

Don't jump to the conclusion from all the above that *Freedom* is a sure shot to be selected over *Enterprise.* The day we were sailing there was a 17 to 18 knot wind and it is in the upper wind range that *Freedom* is at her best. In light air the edge seems to lie with *Enterprise,* though by a narrow margin. In moderate air it appears to be *Freedom* by a whisker. It will therefore be a tough choice, though after a winter of sailing in California, followed by more evaluation when both boats return to Newport one or the other may develop clear dominance. Don't look for a final decision until just before the trials commence in June. As this is written Dennis Conner refuses to make any prediction regarding his ultimate choice and seems defensive of *Enterprise* whenever it is suggested that *Freedom* might be better. Most others who have sailed on both boats throughout the summer and fall of '79 seem very slightly in favor of *Freedom,* but this could change. Dennis claims that his firm intent at the moment is to ensure that no effort be spared to bring both boats to their peak performance. He feels that early favoring of one over the other could result in greater energy being spent on her at the expense of the other, with the possibility of thereby coming to the wrong conclusions and choosing the wrong boat. Since there is no need to make an early choice this seems like a wise course.

Whichever boat he chooses, Dennis Conner and his crew will be very hard to beat. He has proven himself as one of the country's finest sailors, with World Championships in the Star Class to his credit. He was an Olympic medalist in a Tempest in the 1976 games, he has won the Congressional Cup with a perfect record of nine wins in this prestigious match race series. In big boats he has won the SORC and has excelled in the Admiral's Cup series. In 1974 he replaced Ted Turner in the hopeless cause of skippering *Mariner* in the America's Cup trials and got a lot out of her. After *Mariner* was eliminated he became starting helmsman of *Courageous* and it is quite generally agreed he is a past master in match race starts. His greatest attribute is the firm belief that he is going to win the start. While other experienced sailors might become nervous Dennis seems to revel in the challenge of the start and develops a killer instinct. Most sailors are pleased if they see the start developing in such a manner that it will give them a slight edge at the gun. Not Dennis. He uses this as an opportunity to widen the edge and expand it into a wider advantage. Such tactics can backfire and allow the other boat to turn the tables but Dennis doesn't care. He is so supremely confident that he takes that chance in the expectation that he will completely dominate his opponent. He will shout to ruffle the opposition and he is not at all above using the rules to draw the other boat into committing a foul. Cool customers like Ted Turner are not apt to be intimidated, but Conner is not all bluster and confidence. He has a fine sense of timing and distance and is as competent as he is aggressive. Still it is the confidence which gives him the real edge and if his opponents do not get rattled they can get their share of the starts. Conner's aggressiveness on the race course have made him unpopular with some competitors. Between races he is all sweetness and light and cannot understand why he isn't the most popular guy in town. Match racing, he feels, is a dog eat dog affair and he sees nothing wrong in being the meanest dog.

His great confidence could become an Achilles heel if it leads to underestimating the ability of his opponents. For example, as we were running back to Newport against Tom Whidden who had been sailing *Freedom* very well all day (all summer for that matter), Dennis figured out an apparently smart way to catch *Freedom*. She had on a 1½ ounce reaching chute and we were using a three-quarter ounce spinnaker which would be more effective on a run. "Now we will get him," Dennis chortled. "We will hold high, suck him up with us and when we square off for the finish we will kill him."

That's me sailing Courageous *in one of the many close contests against* Intrepid *in 1974. In this situation we crossed with just enough to spare but it wasn't until the last race, with Ted Hood as skipper for the first time, that she finally got the better record in the final trials, to be selected as defender.*

I don't think Dennis ever heard me when I said: "Maybe so, but what if Tom doesn't get sucked up." It turned out that Tom was smart enough not go up with us, and when we bore off belatedly he had doubled his lead. That isn't a big deal because this wasn't a true race but I mention this episode to show the danger of overconfidence. In America's Cup racing it can be very dangerous to assume your opponent is going to do something foolish. He wouldn't be out there if he wasn't smart and concluding that you have a real edge in the thinking department can prove very damaging.

If hard work and dedication can bring victory, Dennis has it won. He gets out on the water early, comes in late. He thinks nothing about sailing every day for months on end. If he and his crew don't get stale in the process (a possibility) this intense effort should prove beneficial. You cannot beat Dennis Conner by working or trying harder. Best to stay cool, have fun and do the best you can. If you are very, very good that approach could work because despite his well deserved reputation as a fine sailor and a particularly fine match racing sailor, Conner is only human.

Like you and me he puts his trousers on one leg at a time.

U.S. 32

Up until November the competition for the defender's role seemed to be between Ted Turner sailing *Courageous* and Dennis Conner sailing either *Enterprise* or *Freedom*. True, Gerry Driscoll was ever hopeful of getting back with *Intrepid.* And then there was another long shot in the form of *Independence,* the 1977 contender designed and sailed by Ted Hood but now under the command of a youngster named Russell Long. In the summer of 1979 Long and his youthful crew sailed *Independence.* She hadn't been good enough in 1977 under more experienced hands but she hadn't been hopeless either. She won some races from *Enterprise* and *Courageous* and when she was losing it was by modest margins. Still she did lose and in match racing being nearly as fast as the opposition presents a pretty hopeless situation.

Still Long and his crew were willing to try and they did a good job, if coming as close as Ted Hood had in losing a couple of years earlier could be considered at all encouraging. They even beat *Courageous* in a few scrub races but far more often they lost, albeit by modest margins. They insisted they would be back in 1980 for the trials—a gallant effort, but one which no one gave any real chance for success. Instead she would be useful mostly for sharpening up *Courageous* in whose camp she lay.

Then in November of 1979 a wonderful thing happened. A large sum of money was raised, but not to back this gallant but almost certainly futile effort to make *Independence* a winner in 1980. Instead it was to be used to build for Long and his crew a brand new boat. All of a sudden there are now not two but three contenders with a real shot at going the distance.

The new boat is not yet named but her number is U. S. 32. She is building at Newport Offshore and will be launched in April of 1980. Johnny Merrifield, formerly of Minneford's, has joined Newport Offshore and will mastermind construction. *Independence* has been scrapped and the new boat is in no way a revamping of her. Her keel will be salvaged but even that will be modified. Also salvaged will be the spars, fittings and winches of *Independence,* all of which are top grade. But these components will be used on a totally new design. Her designer is Dave Pedrick. If that name does not ring any bells it will soon. While employed by Sparkman & Stephens Dave's prime responsibility was to work on the design of *Courageous.* Designs from S&S are team efforts, but no one was more responsible than Pedrick for the superlative boat which emerged. He is just one of several brilliant young designers who were employed by that firm and who have since hung out their own shingle. Dave is confident he can improve on *Courageous.* He is a bit close mouthed as to how, aside from stating he will improve her tacking ability—and *Courageous* was always good in a tacking duel. There is every reason to believe he will come up with a fine Twelve Meter. He is too smart to get sucked into trying for a breakthrough under a rule which defies breakthroughs. But he is also smart enough to recognize the refinements which might work to improve the fine boat *(Courageous)* he worked on six years ago. There is a very real possibility that Russell Long, instead of having to overcome the crippling disadvantage of having a slightly slower boat under his command will have instead the luxury of driving a boat which just might have a minor advantage.

Who is Russell Long? He is first of all the son of Huey Long, whose several *Ondines* have made a big name in ocean racing. Russell cut his eye

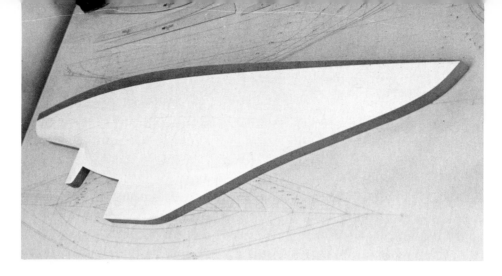

Dave Pedrick's design for 12/US32 reveals nothing startling. She seems a refinement of the very fast Courageous, *as opposed to an ill-advised attempt at a breakthrough. Note that he has elected not to snub her bow.*

teeth racing on them and hence has no dearth of big boat experience. But he has made it on his own, having been one of the top intercollegiate sailors. Fresh out of Harvard, he has done well in several small centerboard classes on a national level. He is a pleasant, yet sensible young man who does not seem at all in awe about sailing against better known sailors for the America's Cup. To assist him he has Andy Rose as tactician, an American who had that role on *Australia* in the 1977 campaign. Also lending mature experience is Dave Vietor as sail trimmer. Dave was for many years a key man at Hood before taking over as the bright young light at Ratsey & Lapthorn. The rest of the crew will be drawn from the able young group which sailed *Independence* in 1979. Now instead of a pretty hopeless cause they have something exciting and potentially rewarding to work with. If their boat is even a fraction faster they could go all the way. Fast boats make smart skippers and Russell Long, though young and relatively inexperienced has proven already that he is both smart and mature beyond his years. Yesterday's prohibitive long shot is now a very real contender.

Dennis Conner, the confident, competent skipper of either Freedom *or* Enterprise *for the 1980 match. Whichever boat he elects to race he is my choice as the pre-match favorite.*

So there you have it—the best group of challengers ever to go after the Cup to be faced by the best group of defenders in its long history. It would be a miracle to be able to pick both the ultimate challenger and defender from this group, let alone the eventual winner of the match. But you now have the lineups and their credentials. How would it grab you to pick Dennis Conner sailing *Freedom* against *Australia,* with the U. S. winning once again, this time very close racing yet with a 4-0 score? If you bet any money on that pairing and outcome you're even crazier than I am in even raising the possibility.

But one thing is certain. America's Cup fever is running high. The greatest yachting event in the world will have its twenty-fourth showing commencing September 16, 1980 off Newport, Rhode Island and the winner will sail to glory.

Appendices
The Official Record of the America's Cup Races
1930-1977

The following details of all the matches from 1930 on are taken directly from the reports of the New York Yacht Club Race Committee. They tell more than just who won or lost each race. Since weather conditions are reported and since the time of each yacht is given at each mark one can ascertain the relative speed of both defender and challenger in different winds and on various points of sailing.

Note, for example, that *Sovereign* which was so badly trounced by *Constellation* in 1964 did gain a full minute on the next to last leg of the last race. She carried a different chute on that leg than in any previous race.

Note also that even that super J-boat *Ranger* lost ground to *Endeavour II* on at least one leg. *Ranger's* greatest superiority was to windward.

The most interesting matches to compare times on are those we nearly lost—1934 and 1970 and to a lesser degree 1962.

The Fourteenth Match 1930 Shamrock V *vs.* Enterprise

First Race—September 13th

Weather, cloudy; Tide, Ebb; Light Fog at start; Clearing before finish; Sea Smooth; Wind at start, N. $\times$ E., 9½ knots; Wind at finish, N.E., 8 knots; Course S. $\times$ W., 15 miles to leeward and return. Distance 30 miles.

	Start 12:55	
	Finish	Elapsed
Shamrock V	5.01.40	4.06.40
Enterprise	4.58.48	4.03.48
	Winner—*Enterprise*	

	Enterprise	*Shamrock V*
Times Rounding, Outer Mark	3.03.19	3.05.15
Elapsed Times, First Leg	2.08.19	2.10.15
Elapsed Times, Second Leg	1.55.29	1.56.25

The start of the race was postponed from 11.40 A.M. to 12.55 P.M. because of fog and lack of wind.

After finishing, each yacht signalled she would race the next week day.

Second Race—September 15th

Weather, clear; Tide, Flood; Light S.E. Ground Swell; Wind at start W.S.W., 7½ knots; Wind at finish, S.W. 10 knots; Course, Triangular, W.S.W.; S.E. $\times$ E.; N. ½ E. Distance 30 miles.

	Start 11:40	
	Finish	Elapsed
Shamrock V	3.50.18	4.10.18
Enterprise	3.40.44	4.00.44
	Winner—*Enterprise*	

	Enterprise	*Shamrock V*
Times Rounding, First Mark	1.20.18	1.26.16
Times Rounding, Second Mark	2.19.28	2.28.31
Elapsed Times, First Leg	1.40.18	1.46.16
Elapsed Times, Second Leg	59.10	1.02.15
Elapsed Times, Third Leg	1.21.16	1.21.47

After finishing, each yacht signalled she would race the next week day.

About one ton of ballast was removed from *Shamrock V* after the first race. Professor Webb certified that this did not change her rating.

SEPTEMBER 16TH

The Race Committee made a trip outside of Newport Harbor at about 10:00 A.M. on the yacht *Javelin.* There was a thick fog and no wind. On returning to the harbor the Committee notified the yachts, *Enterprise* and *Shamrock V;* the larger yachts in the Fleet; the Coast Guard vessels and the sightseeing steamers that the race was called off for the day.

THIRD RACE—SEPTEMBER 17TH

Weather, clear; Tide, Flood; Sea, moderate S.W. Ground Swell; Wind at start, W.S.W., 12 knots; Wind at finish, S.W. 16 knots; Course, W.S.W., 15 miles to windward and return. Distance 30 miles.

Start 11:40

	Finish		Elapsed
Shamrock V		Disabled*	
Enterprise	3.34.16		3.54.16

Winner—*Enterprise*

	Enterprise	*Shamrock V*
Times Rounding, Outer Mark	1.53.33	*
Elapsed Times, First Leg	2.13.33	
Elapsed Times, Second Leg	1.40.43	

*At 12:24 P.M. *Shamrock V* parted main halyard at the masthead sheave. The Race Committee received a radiogram from yacht *Erin* reading:

"Shamrock Will Sail Tomorrow—Colonel Neill"

204

Enterprise signalled she would race the next week day.

About one ton of ballast was replaced in *Shamrock V* after the second race. Professor Webb certified that this did not change her rating.

Fourth Race—September 18th

Weather, clear; Tide, Flood; Sea, light S.W. Ground Swell; Wind at start, W.N.W. 14 knots; at finish, W. 12 knots; Course, Triangular, W.N.W.; S. × E.; N.E. ½ E. Distance 30 miles.

Start 11:40

	Finish	Elapsed
Shamrock V	2.55.57	3.15.57
Enterprise	2.50.13	3.10.13

Winner—*Enterprise*

	Enterprise	*Shamrock V*
Times Rounding, First Mark	1.02.08	1.11.18
Times Rounding, Second Mark	1.54.00	2.01.47
Elapsed Times, First Leg	1.22.08	1.31.18
Elapsed Times, Second Leg	51.52	50.29
Elapsed Times, Third Leg	56.13	54.10

Newport, R. I., September 18, 1930.

George Cormack, Esq.,
    Secretary,
New York Yacht Club,
37 West 44th Street, New York.

Dear Sir:

We have to report that *Enterprise* won "the best four out of seven races" from *Shamrock V* and thereby the Match for the America's Cup.

Edmund Lang, *Chairman*
Colgate Hoyt, *Secretary*
Philip R. Mallory
Race Committee

The Fifteenth Match 1934 Endeavour *vs.* Rainbow

SEPTEMBER 15TH

Weather, Clear; Sea, Smooth; Tidal Current, turned S.×W. at the Lightship at 1:13 P.M. Wind, at start, S.E.×E., 6.8 miles per hour; at 5:10 P.M., S.E.×E., 7 miles per hour. Course, S.E., 15 miles to windward and return. Distance 30 miles.

Start—11:40

	Finish	Elapsed
Endeavour	D.N.F.	
Rainbow	D.N.F.	

	Endeavour	*Rainbow*
Times Rounding Outer Mark	2.46.20	2.43.34
Elapsed Times, First Leg	3.06.20	3.03.34
Elapsed Times, Second Leg		

Each yacht signalled her consent to race the next week day.

Neither yacht finished within the time limit of 5½ hours.

At the expiration of the time limit, *Rainbow* was about a quarter of a mile, and *Endeavour* was about one mile from the finish line.

FIRST RACE—SEPTEMBER 17TH

Weather, Cloudy; Sea, Choppy with moderate swell; Tidal Current, turned N. ×E. at the Lightship at 9:22 A.M. Wind, at start, S.S.E., 16 miles per hour; at finish, S.S.E., 15 miles per hour. Course, S.S.E., 15 miles to windward and return. Distance 30 miles.

Start—11:55

	Finish	Elapsed
Endeavour	3.38.44	3.43.44
Rainbow	3.40.53	3.45.53

Winner—*Endeavour*

	Endeavour	*Rainbow*
Times Rounding Outer Mark	1.59.43	1.59.25
Elapsed Times, First Leg	2.04.43	2.04.25
Elapsed Times, Second Leg	1.39.01	1.41.28

After the course signals had been set the start of this race was postponed fifteen minutes because *Endeavour* was observed to be having difficulty in setting her mainsail, and it was apparent that if the start were not postponed it would result in *Rainbow* having had what would have amounted to a sail-over. In postponing this start the Race Committee was aware that under the agreed conditions of the match it had no power to do so and that such power could only be given it by the joint action of the representative of The Royal Yacht Squadron and The America's Cup Committee. As, however, immediate action by this Committee was imperative, if a sail-over for *Rainbow* was to be averted, this Committee acted as it did in the full confidence that its action would be approved by those having authority to authorize it.

After finishing each yacht signaled her consent to race the next day.

On September 16th *Endeavour* removed 1100 lbs. of ballast. Dr. Webb certified that this did not change her rating.

SECOND RACE—SEPTEMBER 18TH

Weather, Cloudy; Sea, Moderate swell; Tidal Current, turned N.×E. at the Lightship at 10:32 A.M. Wind, at start, N.W., 14 miles per hour; at finish, N.W., 9.5 miles per hour. Course, Triangular, S.×W., N.W., E.N.E. ½E. Distance 30 miles.

Start—11:40

	Finish	Elapsed
Endeavour	2.49.01	3.09.01
Rainbow	2.49.52	3.09.52

Winner—*Endeavour*

	Endeavour	*Rainbow*
Times Rounding, First Mark	12.36.37	12.36.53
Times Rounding, Second Mark	1.54.56	1.56.27
Elapsed Times, First Leg	0.56.37	0.56.53
Elapsed Times, Second Leg	1.18.19	1.19.34
Elapsed Times, Third Leg	0.54.05	0.53.25

After finishing each yacht signalled her consent to race the next day.

September 19th

Both yachts appeared at the starting line but on account of lack of wind, the Committee boat hoisted the signal "H" at 1:20 P.M. calling the race off for the day.

Third Race—September 20th

Weather, Partly Cloudy; Sea, Smooth; Tidal Current, turned N.×E. at the Lightship at 12:37 P.M. Wind, at start, N.E.×E., 6.2 miles per hour; at finish, S.E.×S., 8.8 miles per hour. Course, S.W.×W., 15 miles to leeward and return. Distance 30 miles.

Start—11:40

	Finish	Elapsed
Rainbow	4.15.34	4.35.34
Endeavour	4.19.00	4.39.00

Winner—Rainbow

	Endeavour	*Rainbow*
Times Rounding Outer Mark	2.00.38	2.07.17
Elapsed Times, First Leg	2.20.38	2.27.17
Elapsed Times, Second Leg	2.18.22	2.08.17

After finishing *Rainbow* signalled her consent to race the next day.
Endeavour signalled she would not race the next day.
On September 19th *Endeavour* removed 3360 lbs. of ballast. Dr. Webb certified that this did not change her rating.

Fourth Race—September 22nd

Weather, Cloudy; Sea, Choppy with light swell; Tidal Current, turned N.×E. at the Lightship at 2:25 P.M. Wind, at start, E., 11.5 miles per hour; at finish, E.×S.,

12.5 miles per hour. Course, Triangular, E., S.W.×S., N.N.W.½W. Distance 30 miles.

Start—11:40

	Finish	Elapsed
Rainbow	2.55.38	3.15.38
Endeavour	2.56.53	3.16.53

Winner—*Rainbow*

	Rainbow	*Endeavour*
Times Rounding, First Mark	1.05.48	1.05.25
Times Rounding, Second Mark	2.00.35	2.01.35
Elapsed Times, First Leg	1.25.48	1.25.25
Elapsed Times, Second Leg	0.54.47	0.56.10
Elapsed Times, Third Leg	0.55.03	0.55.18

After finishing each yacht signalled her consent to race the next weekday.

On September 21st *Rainbow* added 4000 lbs. of ballast. Dr. Webb certified that this did not change her rating.

Endeavour displayed Protest Flag.

Fifth Race—September 24th

Weather, Cloudy; Sea, Short Chop; Tidal Current, turned N.×E. at the Lightship at 4:02 P.M. Wind, at start, N.E.×N., 14 miles per hour; at finish, N.E.×N., 18.5 miles per hour. Course, S.W.×S., 15 miles to leeward and return. Distance 30 miles.

Start—11:40

	Finish	Elapsed
Rainbow	3.34.05	3.54.05
Endeavour	3.38.06	3.58.06

Winner—*Rainbow*

	Rainbow	*Endeavour*
Times Rounding, First Mark	1.18.37	1.23.15
Elapsed Times, First Leg	1.38.37	1.43.15
Elapsed Times, Second Leg	2.15.28	2.14.51

After finishing each yacht signalled her consent to race the next weekday.

On September 23rd *Rainbow* added 1000 lbs. of ballast.

On September 23rd *Endeavour* added 3360 lbs. of ballast.

Dr. Webb certified that this additional ballast did not change the rating of either yacht.

Sixth Race—September 25th

Weather, Partly cloudy; Sea, Light swell; Tidal Current, turned N.×E. at the Lightship at 4:51 P.M. Wind, at start, N.E., 9.5 miles per hour; at finish, 12.5 miles per hour. Course, Triangular, S.×E., N.E., W.N.W.½W. Distance 30 miles.

Start—11:40

	Finish	Elapsed
Rainbow	3.20.05	3.40.05
Endeavour	3.21.00	3.41.00

Winner—Rainbow

	Rainbow	*Endeavour*
Times Rounding, First Mark	12.52.59	12.51.50
Times Rounding, Second Mark	2.12.28	2.15.12
Times Rounding, Third Mark	3.20.05	3.21.00
Elapsed Times, First Leg	1.12.59	1.11.50
Elapsed Times, Second Leg	1.19.29	1.23.22
Elapsed Times, Third Leg	1.07.37	1.05.48

Rainbow and *Endeavour* both displayed Protest Flags at the start. Both protests were withdrawn after the race.

Newport, R. I., September 25, 1934.

George A. Cormack, Esq.,
  Secretary,
New York Yacht Club,
37 West 44th Street, New York.

Dear Sir:

We have to report that *Rainbow* won "the best four out of seven races" from *Endeavour* and thereby the Match for the America's Cup.

> Edmund Lang, *Chairman*
> E. Vail Stebbins, *Secretary*
> Clinton Mackenzie
> Race Committee

The Sixteenth Match 1937 Endeavour II vs. Ranger

FIRST RACE—JULY 31ST

Weather, Cloudy, moderate fog at finish; Sea, Smooth; Tidal Current, turned north at Brenton Reef Lightship at 8:29 A.M. Wind at start, S. × E., 5 miles per hour; at 6:06 P.M. S.E. × S., 10.5 miles per hour. Course S. × E., 15 miles to windward and return. Distance 30 miles.

Start—1:25

	Finish	Elapsed
Ranger	6.06.15	4.41.15
Endeavour II	6.23.20	4.58.20

Winner—*Ranger*

	Ranger	Endeavour II
Times Rounding Outer Mark	4.14.49	4.21.03
Elapsed Times, First Leg	2.49.49	2.56.03
Elapsed Times, Second Leg	1.51.26	2.02.17

There were three 15 minute postponements because of lack of wind and to give the Coast Guard time to clear the starting line.

Each yacht signalled her consent to race the next week day.

Second Race—August 2nd

Weather, Clear overhead, fog haze on surface; Sea, Smooth; Tidal Current, turned North at Brenton Reef Lightship at 10:49 A.M. Wind at start, S.W., 8.2 miles per hour; at 4:21 P.M. S.W., 11.5 miles per hour. Course triangular, S.W., E.×S., N.×W.½ W. Distance 30 miles.

Start—12:40

	Finish	Elapsed
Ranger	4.21.33	3.41.33
Endeavour II	4.40.05	4.00.05

Winner—*Ranger*

	Ranger	*Endeavour II*
Times Rounding First Mark	2.26.57	2.37.25
Times Rounding Second Mark	3.27.20	3.43.39
Elapsed Times, First Leg	1.46.57	1.57.25
Elapsed Times, Second Leg	1.00.23	1.06.14
Elapsed Times, Third Leg	0.54.13	0.56.26

After finishing *Endeavour II* requested one day postponement, which was immediately granted. *Ranger* signalled her consent to race the next week day.

Third Race—August 4th

Weather, Clear overhead, fog haze on surface; Sea, Short chop; Tidal Current, turned North at Brenton Reef Lightship at 12:59 P.M. Wind at start, S.W., 11.5 miles per hour; at 4:34 P.M., S.W., 12.5 miles per hour. Course, S.W., 15 miles to windward and return. Distance 30 miles.

Start—12:40

	Finish	Elapsed
Ranger	4.34.30	3.54.30
Endeavour II	4.38.57	3.58.57

Winner—*Ranger*

	Ranger	*Endeavour II*
Times Rounding Outer Mark	2.43.45	2.47.58
Elapsed Times, First Leg	2.03.45	2.07.58
Elapsed Times, Second Leg	1.50.45	1.50.59

After finishing each yacht signalled her consent to race the next week day.

On August 3rd *Endeavour II* removed 5080 lbs. of ballast. Dr. Webb certified that this did not change her rating.

FOURTH RACE—AUGUST 5TH

Weather, Clear; Sea, Smooth; Tidal Current, turned North at Brenton Reef Lightship at 2:58 P.M. Wind, at start, S.W., 12.5 miles per hour; at 3:47 P.M., S.W., 16 miles per hour. Course triangular, S.W., E.×S., N.×W. ½ W. Distance 30 miles.

Start—12:40

	Finish	Elapsed
Ranger	3.47.49	3.07.49
Endeavour II	3.51.26	3.11.26

Winner—*Ranger*

	Ranger	*Endeavour II*
Times Rounding First Mark	1.57.45	2.01.50
Times Rounding Second Mark	2.54.51	2.58.26
Elapsed Times, First Leg	1.17.45	1.21.50
Elapsed Times, Second Leg	0.57.06	0.56.36
Elapsed Times, Third Leg	0.52.58	0.53.00

At the start *Endeavour II* crossed the starting line nine seconds early and was recalled. She recrossed one minute and fifteen seconds after the starting signal.

Newport, R. I., August 5, 1937.

George A. Cormack, Esq.,
  Secretary,
New York Yacht Club,
37 West 44th Street, New York.

Dear Sir:

We have to report that *Ranger* won "the best four out of seven races" from *Endeavour II* and thereby the Match for the America's Cup.

Edmund Lang, *Chairman*
Walter L. Coursen, *Secretary*
George M. Pynchon
Race Committee

The Seventeenth Match 1958 Sceptre *vs.* Columbia

FIRST RACE—SEPTEMBER 20TH

Course: Windward-Leeward Twice Around
     Distance 24.0 miles

Wind: North ½ East 8 m.p.h.

Actual Time of Start	*Columbia*	12:30:10
Actual Time of Start	*Sceptre*	12:30:11
Time at First Mark	*Columbia*	13:54:41
Time at First Mark	*Sceptre*	14:02:17
Time at Second Mark	*Columbia*	15:47:16
Time at Second Mark	*Sceptre*	15:49:43
Time at Third Mark	*Columbia*	16:42:38
Time at Third Mark	*Sceptre*	16:50:10
Time at Finish	*Columbia*	17:43:56
Time at Finish	*Sceptre*	17:51:40

Winner—*Columbia*

Second Race—September 22nd

Course: Triangular
           Distance 24.0 miles

Wind: North ½ East 7 m.p.h.

Actual Time of Start	*Columbia*	12:21:32
Actual Time of Start	*Sceptre*	12:21:34
Time at First Mark	*Sceptre*	15:46:16
Time at First Mark	*Columbia*	15:48:01
Time at Second Mark	*Columbia*	16:52:04
Time at Second Mark	*Sceptre*	16:52:54

No race. Time limit expired at 17:50:00.
  Sceptre signaled her unwillingness to start the next day.

Third Race—September 25th

Course: Windward-Leeward Twice Around
           Distance 24.0 miles

Wind: South West by West ¼ West 15 to 20 m.p.h.

Actual Time of Start	*Sceptre*	12:10:04
Actual Time of Start	*Columbia*	12:10:05
Time at First Mark	*Columbia*	13:09:28
Time at First Mark	*Sceptre*	13:11:51
Time at Second Mark	*Columbia*	13:45:27
Time at Second Mark	*Sceptre*	13:47:56
Time at Third Mark	*Columbia*	14:43:22
Time at Third Mark	*Sceptre*	14:51:07
Time at Finish	*Columbia*	15:19:07
Time at Finish	*Sceptre*	15:27:27

Winner—*Columbia*

Fourth Race—September 26th

Course: Triangular
        Distance 24.0 miles

Wind: South West by West 12 to 17 m.p.h.

Actual Time of Start	*Columbia*	12:10:10
Actual Time of Start	*Sceptre*	12:10:23
Time at First Mark	*Columbia*	13:28:44
Time at First Mark	*Sceptre*	13:34:14
Time at Second Mark	*Columbia*	14:20:31
Time at Second Mark	*Sceptre*	14:28:44
Time at Finish	*Columbia*	15:14:22
Time at Finish	*Sceptre*	15:21:27

Winner—*Columbia*

At the start *Sceptre* crossed the starting line two seconds early and was recalled. She recrossed twenty-three seconds after the starting signal.

Newport, R.I., September 26, 1958

W. Mahlon Dickerson, Esq.,
    Secretary
New York Yacht Club,
37 West 44th Street, New York

Dear Sir:

The New York Yacht Club Race Committee reports that *Columbia* won "the best four out of seven races" from *Sceptre* and thereby the Match for the America's Cup.

John S. Dickerson, Jr., Chairman
Race Committee

The Eighteenth Match 1962 Gretel vs. Weatherly

FIRST RACE—SEPTEMBER 15TH

Course: Windward-Leeward Twice Around
   Distance 24.0 miles

Wind: 290 degrees—10 knots

Actual Time of Start	*Weatherly*	13:10:12
Actual Time of Start	*Gretel*	13:10:26
Time at First Mark	*Weatherly*	14:08:02
Time at First Mark	*Gretel*	14:09:37
Time at Second Mark	*Weatherly*	14:47:51
Time at Second Mark	*Gretel*	14:49:03
Time at Third Mark	*Weatherly*	15:42:58
Time at Third Mark	*Gretel*	15:46:16
Time at Finish	*Weatherly*	16:23:57
Time at Finish	*Gretel*	16:27:43

Winner—*Weatherly*

Gretel signaled her unwillingness to start the next day.

SECOND RACE—SEPTEMBER 18

Course: Triangular
   Distance 24.0 miles

Wind: 285 degrees—20–25 knots

Actual Time of Start	*Gretel*	12:20:11
Actual Time of Start	*Weatherly*	12:20:17
Time at First Mark	*Weatherly*	13:31:06
Time at First Mark	*Gretel*	13:31:18
Time at Second Mark	*Weatherly*	14:18:47
Time at Second Mark	*Gretel*	14:19:01
Time at Finish	*Gretel*	15:06:58
Time at Finish	*Weatherly*	15:07:45

Winner—*Gretel*

Gretel signaled her unwillingness to start the next day.

Third Race—September 20th

Course: Windward-Leeward Twice Around
        Distance 24.0 miles

Wind: 010 degrees—9-12 knots

Actual Time of Start	*Gretel*	12:50:21
Actual Time of Start	*Weatherly*	12:50:24
Time at First Mark	*Weatherly*	14:00:04
Time at First Mark	*Gretel*	14:01:02
Time at Second Mark	*Weatherly*	15:10:28
Time at Second Mark	*Gretel*	15:33:45
Time at Third Mark	*Weatherly*	16:18:24
Time at Third Mark	*Gretel*	16:33:40
Time at Finish	*Weatherly*	17:11:16
Time at Finish	*Gretel*	17:19:56

Winner—*Weatherly*

Gretel signaled her unwillingness to start the next day.

Fourth Race—September 22nd

Course: Triangular
        Distance 24.0 miles

Wind: 175 degrees—8-10 knots

Actual Time of Start	*Weatherly*	13:05:19
Actual Time of Start	*Gretel*	13:05:23
Time at First Mark	*Weatherly*	14:34:55
Time at First Mark	*Gretel*	14:36:21

Time at Second Mark	*Weatherly*	15:31:25
Time at Second Mark	*Gretel*	15:32:13
Time at Finish	*Weatherly*	16:27:28
Time at Finish	*Gretel*	16:27:54

Winner—*Weatherly*

Gretel signaled her unwillingness to start the next day.

FIFTH RACE—SEPTEMBER 25TH

Course: Windward-Leeward Twice Around
      Distance 24.0 miles

Wind: 245 degrees—8-10 knots

Actual Time of Start	*Gretel*	13:10:09
Actual Time of Start	*Weatherly*	13:10:13
Time at First Mark	*Weatherly*	14:07:05
Time at First Mark	*Gretel*	14:09:09
Time at Second Mark	*Weatherly*	14:46:50
Time at Second Mark	*Gretel*	14:49:18
Time at Third Mark	*Weatherly*	15:46:01
Time at Third Mark	*Gretel*	15:49:40
Time at Finish	*Weatherly*	16:26:17
Time at Finish	*Gretel*	16:29:57

Winner—*Weatherly*

Newport, R.I., September 25, 1962

W. Mahlon Dickerson, Esq.,
    Secretary
New York Yacht Club,
37 West 44th Street, New York

Dear Sir:

The New York Yacht Club Race Committee reports that *Weatherly* won "the best four out of seven races" from *Gretel* and thereby the Match for the America's Cup.

Julian K. Roosevelt, *Chairman*
Race Committee

The Nineteenth Match 1964 Sovereign vs. Constellation

FIRST RACE—SEPTEMBER 15TH

Course: America's Cup Course—24.3 Miles
Wind at Start: W × S—6-8 Knots

Times	Sovereign	Constellation
Start	12:35:00	12:35:00
1st Mark	13:19:20	13:17:31
2nd Mark	13:41:31	13:39:36
3rd Mark	14:05:03	14:03:13
4th Mark	14:49:11	14:46:11
5th Mark	15:27:47	15:22:56
Finish	16:11:15	16:05:41

SECOND RACE—SEPTEMBER 16TH

Race postponed—due to insufficient and variable winds.

SECOND RACE—SEPTEMBER 17TH

Course: America's Cup Course—24.3 Miles
Wind at Start: SSW—15-17 Knots

Times	Sovereign	Constellation
Start	12:10:00	12:10:00
1st Mark	13:02:05	12:58:22
2nd Mark	13:24:04	13:20:32
3rd Mark	13:45:00	13:41:38
4th Mark	14:36:16	14:30:55
5th Mark	15:18:41	15:06:13
Finish	16:17:12	15:56:48

Sovereign signaled her unwillingness to start the next day.

Third Race—September 19th

Course: America's Cup Course—24.3 Miles
Wind at Start: E ½ N—15-17 Knots

Times	Sovereign	Constellation
Start	12:10:00	12:10:00
1st Mark	13:03:10	12:59:03
2nd Mark	13:26:07	13:21:38
3rd Mark	13:45:56	13:41:23
4th Mark	14:34:39	14:29:07
5th Mark	15:04:36	14:58:47
Finish	15:54:40	15:48:07

Fourth Race—September 21st

Course: America's Cup Course—24.3 Miles
Wind at Start: E × N—8 Knots

Times	Sovereign	Constellation
Start	12:10:00	12:10:00
1st Mark	13:08:58	13:04:11
2nd Mark	13:37:43	13:32:22
3rd Mark	14:00:20	13:53:57
4th Mark	15:01:20	14:47:54
5th Mark	15:42:25	15:29:59
Finish	16:38:07	16:22:27

Newport, R. I., September 21, 1964

Arthur J. Santry, Jr., Esq.
New York Yacht Club,
37 West 44th Street, New York

Dear Sir:

The New York Yacht Club Race Committee reports that *Constellation* won "the best four out of seven races" from *Sovereign* and thereby the Match for the America's Cup.

F. Briggs Dalzell, *Chairman*
Race Committee

The Twentieth Match *1967* Dame Pattie *vs.* Intrepid

First Race—September 12th

Wind at Start—E×N¼N, 18 Knots . . . Wind at Finish—E×N¼N, 15 Knots

	Intrepid		*Dame Pattie*
Official Start		12:30:00	
Actual Start	12:30:16		12:30:06
1st Mark	13:15:45		13:17:35
2nd Mark	13:35:57		13:38:08
3rd Mark	13:52:40		13:55:30
4th Mark	14:39:07		14:43:33
5th Mark	15:08:56		15:14:02
Finish	15:55:03		16:01:01
Margin		00:05:58	

Second Race—September 13th

Wind at Start—E×N¼N, 7 Knots . . . Wind at Finish—E×N¼N, 11–14 Knots

	Intrepid		*Dame Pattie*
Official Start		12:35:00	
Actual Start	12:35:15		12:35:14
1st Mark	13:22:09		13:23:02
2nd Mark	13:45:22		13:46:54
3rd Mark	14:03:24		14:05:27
4th Mark	14:48:23		14:50:19
5th Mark	15:20:49		15:24:12
Finish	16:04:21		16:07:57
Margin		00:03:36	

THIRD RACE—SEPTEMBER 14TH

Wind at Start—NE×E, 12 Knots . . . Wind at Finish—NE½E, 16 Knots

	Intrepid		Dame Pattie
Official Start		12:20:00	
Actual Start	12:20:07		12:20:06
1st Mark	13:04:29		13:05:50
2nd Mark	13:24:49		13:26:09
3rd Mark	13:44:15		13:45:59
4th Mark	14:28:10		14:31:30
5th Mark	14:58:11		15:01:46
Finish	15:40:14		15:44:55
Margin		00:03:41	

Dame Pattie signalled her unwillingness to start the next day.

SEPTEMBER 16TH

—Race postponed due to hurricane Doria.

September 17th

—Race postponed due to fog.

FOURTH RACE—SEPTEMBER 18TH

Wind at Start—SW, 12 Knots . . . Wind at Finish—SW×W, 8 Knots

	Intrepid		Dame Pattie
Official Start		14:00:00	
Actual Start	14:00:04		14:00:01
1st Mark	14:42:59		14:44:24
2nd Mark	15:03:07		15:04:59
3rd Mark	15:23:28		15:25:46
4th Mark	16:05:58		16:09:52
5th Mark	16:45:18		16:47:43
Finish	17:27:39		17:31:14
Margin		00:03:35	

Newport, R.I., September 18, 1967

Donald B. Kipp, Esq.
New York Yacht Club,
37 West 44th Street, New York

Dear Sir:

The New York Yacht Club Race Committee reports that *Intrepid* won "the best four of seven races" from *Dame Pattie* and thereby the Match for the America's Cup.

Henry H. Anderson, Jr., *Chairman*
Race Committee

The Twenty-First Match 1970 Gretel II *vs.* Intrepid

First Race—September 15th

Wind at Start—109˚, 20 K . . . at Finish—110˚, 12–15 K

	Intrepid	*Gretel II*	*Margins*	*Leader*
Actual Start	12:10:06	12:10:08	00:02	*Intrepid*
1st Mark	12:49:33	12:50:36	01:03	"
2nd Mark	13:11:17	13:12:25	01:08	"
3rd Mark	13:30:19	13:33:46	03:27	"
4th Mark	14:15:49	14:20:00	04:11	"
5th Mark	14:54:23	15:00:38	06:15	"
Finish	15:36:03	15:41:55	05:52	"

The weather mark was shifted 15˚ to starboard after the first leg.
Protests of both yachts before the start were disallowed.
Gretel II signalled her unwillingness to start the next day.

September 17th

—Race postponed due to lack of wind.

Second Race—September 18th

Wind at Start—201°, 9 K

	Gretel II	Intrepid	Margins	Leader
Actual Start	12:30:08	12:30:11	00:03	Gretel II
1st Mark	13:18:42	13:20:36	01:54	"
2nd Mark	13:47:13	13:47:33	00:20	"
3rd Mark	14:12:04	14:11:18	00:46	Intrepid

Race was abandoned after 3rd mark at 1452 hours due to thickening fog. *Gretel II* signalled her unwillingness to start the next day.

Second Race—September 20th

Wind at Start—238°, 6 K . . . at Finish—226°, 9 K

	Gretel II	Intrepid	Margins	Leader
Official Start	14:00:00			
Actual Start	Not Recorded			
1st Mark	15:08:33	15:07:51	00:42	Intrepid
2nd Mark	15:35:13	15:34:04	01:09	"
3rd Mark	15:58:32	15:56:50	01:42	"
4th Mark	16:54:28	16:53:16	01:12	"
5th Mark	17:44:29	17:45:19	00:50	Gretel II
Finish	18:37:03	18:38:10	01:07	"

Gretel II was disqualified for a foul after the starting signal and the race was awarded to *Intrepid.*

Both yachts signalled their unwillingness to start the next day.

THIRD RACE—SEPTEMBER 22ND

Wind at Start—236°, 10 K . . . at Finish—230°, 18 K

	Intrepid	Gretel II	Margins	Leader
Actual Start	12:10:09	12:10:14	00:05	Intrepid
1st Mark	12:53:42	12:54:28	00:46	"
2nd Mark	13:14:35	13:15:21	00:46	"
3rd Mark	13:36:47	13:37:43	00:56	"
4th Mark	14:20:27	14:21:20	00:53	"
5th Mark	14:53:56	14:55:12	01:16	"
Finish	15:34:43	15:36:01	01:18	"

Both yachts signalled their unwillingness to start the next day.

FOURTH RACE—SEPTEMBER 24TH

Wind at Start—076°, 10 K . . . at Finish—120°, 4-6 K

	Gretel II	Intrepid	Margins	Leader
Actual Start	12:10:21	12:10:13	00:08	Intrepid
1st Mark	12:54:56	12:54:27	00:29	"
2nd Mark	13:15:53	13:15:29	00:24	"
3rd Mark	13:36:52	13:36:12	00:40	"
4th Mark	14:19:52	14:18:56	00:56	"
5th Mark	14:52:25	14:51:23	01:02	"
Finish	15:33:59	15:35:01	01:02	Gretel II

Intrepid signalled her unwillingness to start the next day.

SEPTEMBER 26TH

—Race postponed due to fog. *Intrepid* signalled her unwillingness to start the next day.

Fifth Race—September 28th

Wind at Start—360°, 9-10 K . . . at Finish—045°, 5 K

	Intrepid	Gretel II	Margins	Leader
Actual Start	12:10:11	12:10:10	00:01	Gretel II
1st Mark	12:56:47	12:57:31	00:44	Intrepid
2nd Mark	13:29:14	13:29:54	00:40	"
3rd Mark	13:58:39	13:59:18	00:39	"
4th Mark	14:55:25	14:56:16	00:51	"
5th Mark	15:55:22	15:55:42	00:20	"
Finish	16:39:03	16:40:47	01:44	"

The Twenty-Second Match 1974 Southern Cross vs. Courageous

First Race—September 10th

Course: America's Cup Course. Bearing to first mark 212°. Bearing to fourth and finish marks changed to 225°. Distance 24.3 miles.
Wind: At Start 212°, 11 knots. At Finish 222°, 7 knots.

	Courageous	Southern Cross	Margins
Official Start		14:10	
Actual Start	14:10:06	14:10:08	00:02
1st Mark	14:52:32	14:53:06	00:34
2nd Mark	15:18:15	15:19:37	01:22
3rd Mark	15:38:25	15:39:58	01:33
4th Mark	16:27:30	16:30:40	03:10
5th Mark	17:25:30	17:29:35	04:05
Finish	18:22:03	18:26:57	04:54
Elapsed Time	04:12:03	04:16:57	

Both yachts signalled their willingness to start the next day.

SEPTEMBER 11TH

—The second race was postponed to a later date because of lack of wind. Both yachts signalled their willingness to start the next day.

SECOND RACE—SEPTEMBER 12TH

Course: America's Cup Course. Bearing to first mark 237˚. Distance 24.3 miles. Wind: At Start 237˚, 11 knots. At Finish 236˚, 16 knots.

	Courageous	*Southern Cross*	*Margins*
Official Start		12:10	
Actual Start	12:10:09	12:10:08	00:01
1st Mark	12:55:00	12:55:34	00:34
2nd Mark	13:17:54	13:18:22	00:28
3rd Mark	13:39:54	13:40:28	00:34
4th Mark	14:24:27	14:25:23	00:56
5th Mark	14:59:55	15:00:40	00:45
Finish	15:42:37	15:43:48	01:11
Elapsed Time	03:32:37	03:33:48	

Both yachts finished with protest flags displayed.

Both yachts signalled their willingness to start the next day.

September 13th—Course Signals for Race 3 were hoisted at 11:50, however the race was postponed at 12:00 because of fog.

Both yachts signalled their willingness to start the next day.

September 14th—Race 3 was started but due to light wind neither yacht finished within the time limit which expired at 17:40.

Southern Cross requested a layover day the next day.

THIRD RACE—SEPTEMBER 16TH

Course: America's Cup Course. Bearing to first mark 300°. Bearing to Finish mark changed to 310°. Distance 24.3 miles.
Wind: At Start 305°, 12 knots. At Finish 308°, 11 knots.

	Courageous	Southern Cross	Margins
Official Start		12:10	
Actual Start	12:11:01	12:11:17	00:16
1st Mark	12:56:19	12:57:04	00:45
2nd Mark	13:18:49	13:20:14	01:25
3rd Mark	13:42:08	13:43:24	01:16
4th Mark	14:26:57	14:29:49	02:52
5th Mark	15:00:45	15:04:17	03:32
Finish	15:43:02	15:48:29	05:27
Elapsed Time	03:33:02	03:38:29	

Both yachts signalled their willingness to start the next day.

FOURTH RACE—SEPTEMBER 17TH

Course: America's Cup Course. Bearing to first mark 190°. Bearing to fourth mark changed to 215°. Distance 24.3 miles.
Wind: At Start 190°, 12 knots. At Finish 214°, 12 knots.

	Courageous	Southern Cross	Margins
Official Start		12:10	
Actual Start	12:10:07	12:10:27	00:20
1st Mark	12:51:51	12:53:10	01:19
2nd Mark	13:16:26	13:18:06	01:40
3rd Mark	13:38:20	13:40:09	01:49
4th Mark	14:22:20	14:26:22	04:02
5th Mark	14:59:23	15:03:53	04:30
Finish	15:42:25	15:49:44	07:19
Elapsed Time	03:32:25	03:39:44	

Courageous is the winner of the America's Cup.

The Twenty-Third Match 1977 Australia *vs.* Courageous

FIRST RACE—SEPTEMBER 13TH

America's Cup Course 24.3 miles. Weather leg 4.5 miles, 225 degrees.

Official Start 12:10:00

Yachts	Australia	Courageous	Deltas	Wind
Start	12:10:12	12:10:24	00:12 (A)	225, 12.5 k
1st Mark			01:08 (C)	
2nd Mark			01:16 (C)	
3rd Mark			01:23 (C)	
4th Mark			01:12 (C)	
5th Mark			01:18 (C)	
Finish			01:48 (C)	205, 17 k

The weather mark was moved for the 6th leg to 205 degrees.
Australia requested a lay day the next day.

SECOND RACE—SEPTEMBER 15TH

America's Cup Course 24.3 miles. Weather leg 4.5 miles, 050 degrees.

Official Start 12:10:00

Yachts	Australia	Courageous	Deltas	Wind
Start	12:10:06	12:10:07	00:01 (A)	050, 10 k
1st Mark	12:57:46	12:56:58	00:48 (C)	
2nd Mark	13:30:17	13:29:57	00:20 (C)	
3rd Mark	13:55:32	13:54:48	00:44 (C)	
4th Mark	15:13:51	15:03:06	10:45 (C)	
5th Mark	16:22:17	16:16:40	05:37 (C)	
Finish			At time limit.	125, 3 k

The weather mark was moved for the 4th leg to 110 degrees.
The time limit expired with *Courageous* approximately 570 yards and *Australia* approximately 2,280 yards from the finish.

Second Race—September 16th

America's Cup Course 24.3 miles. Weather leg 4.5 miles, 190 degrees.

Official Start 12:10:00

Yachts	Australia	Courageous	Deltas	Wind
Start	12:10:03	12:10:02	00:01 (C)	195, 11 k
1st Mark	13:00:06	12:58:06	02:00 (C)	
2nd Mark	13:21:57	13:19:57	02:00 (C)	
3rd Mark	13:50:33	13:47:55	02:38 (C)	
4th Mark	14:32:20	14:30:12	02:08 (C)	
5th Mark	15:11:46	15:10:40	01:06 (C)	
Finish	15:55:10	15:54:07	01:03 (C)	160, 15 k

The weather mark was moved for the 4th leg.

Third Race—September 17th

America's Cup Course 24.3 miles. Weather leg 4.5 miles, 240 degrees.

Official Start 12:10:00

Yachts	Australia	Courageous	Deltas	Wind
Start	12:10:21	12:10:15	00:12 (C)	238, 8 k
1st Mark	13:02:44	13:00:54	01:50 (C)	
2nd Mark	13:42:33	13:40:02	02:31 (C)	
3rd Mark	14:08:41	14:05:37	03:04 (C)	275, 9–10 k
4th Mark	14:59:12	14:55:45	03:27 (C)	
5th Mark	15:42:33	15:40:36	01:57 (C)	
Finish	16:35:55	16:33:23	02:32 (C)	310, 8 k

The weather mark was moved for the 4th leg to 275 degrees.

Fourth Race—September 18th

America's Cup Course 24.3 miles. Weather leg 4.5 miles, 265 degrees.

Official Start 12:10:00

Yachts	Australia	Courageous	Deltas	Wind
Start	12:10:09	12:10:09	00:00	265, 14 k
1st Mark	12:54:16	12:53:32	00:44 (C)	
2nd Mark	13:14:34	13:13:46	00:48 (C)	
3rd Mark	13:34:54	13:33:58	00:56 (C)	
4th Mark	14:19:12	14:17:01	02:11 (C)	
5th Mark	15:01:17	14:58:42	02:35 (C)	
Finish	15:44:56	15:42:31	02:25 (C)	260, 9 k

Courageous successfully defended the Cup by winning four straight races. After the Race, in reply to the hoist CHARLIE-UNIFORM-EIGHT-ZERO, both yachts signalled "Affirmative".

The Conditions of the 1980 Match

The Conditions which shall govern the races for the America's Cup under the challenge of the Yacht Club d'Hyeres, dated May 9, 1978, for a Match in the International Twelve Metre Class, as agreed by the Committees of the Yacht Club d'Hyeres and the New York Yacht Club, are as follows:

Note: Wherever time is referred to in these Conditions, it is Eastern Daylight Time.

1. *Date of Races:*

   The first race shall be sailed on September 16, 1980, and the races shall be sailed on every succeeding day; provided, however, that immediately at the conclusion of each race or upon a race being postponed for the day or abandoned the Race Committee shall inquire of each contestant whether he is willing to start the next day, and each contestant shall reply within one hour. Should either contestant reply in the negative, one day shall intervene before starting the next race.

   However, each contestant shall only be entitled to request two lay days in the course of the Match, except that a third day may be requested by each contestant after four races have been completed.

2. *Number of Races:*
The Match shall be decided by the best four out of seven races.

3. *Courses:*
Races shall start at the America's Cup Buoy anchored 7.9 nautical miles 150 degrees (Magnetic) from the Brenton Reef Light and shall be approximately 24 3/10 nautical miles in length.

Races shall consist of six legs. The first leg, to be approximately 4½ nautical miles in length, shall be from the starting buoy to a mark to windward; the second leg shall be from the first mark to a mark equidistant from the starting buoy and the first mark at a point on the circumference of a circle the diameter of which is the first leg; the third leg shall be from the second mark back to the starting buoy; the fourth leg shall be from the starting buoy to the first mark; the fifth leg shall be from the first mark to the starting buoy; and the sixth leg shall be from the starting buoy to the first mark, at which the finish line shall be established.

Marks are to be left on the same hand as the starting mark (America's Cup Buoy) except as modified by the Sailing Instructions.

The Magnetic course of the first leg shall be signalled, and the mark vessel shall be started not less than 10 minutes prior to the warning signal.

The various rounds of the course will resemble the diagram on page 235.

There shall be included in the Sailing Instructions detailed arrangements for moving the weather mark after the first leg, in the event of a shift of wind, for either or both the fourth and sixth legs.

Under no circumstances may this course be shortened.

4. *Start:*
The warning signal, unless the race is postponed by the Race Committee, shall be made as nearly as practicable at 1200; and the starting signal, at 1210. No race shall be started after 1410. In the event that a race or races are to be held on September 28 and thereafter, the warning signal shall be made as nearly as practicable at 1100 and the starting signal, at 1110; and no race shall be started after 1310.

5. *Signals:*
The warning signal shall be made ten minutes before the start.

Five minutes after the warning signal the preparatory signal shall be made. Five minutes after the preparatory signal the starting signal shall be made. The time of the starting signal shall be taken as the time of the start of both yachts.

Diagram of Course

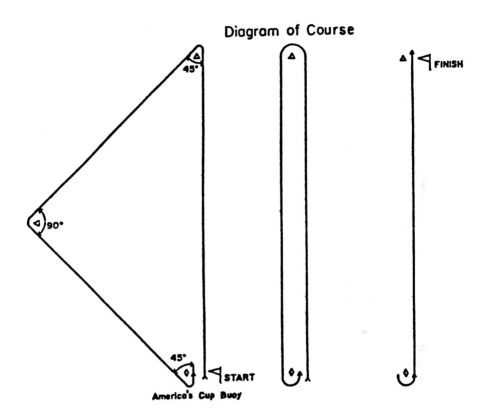

6. Yachts shall stay outside of the starting marks on their assigned end of the starting line prior to the warning signal and are obliged to enter the starting area from the course side of the starting line after the warning signal.

Assignments shall be by a coin flip prior to the first race of the Match and positions will alternate for each race thereafter.

Yachts violating this instruction are subject to protest by the Race Committee only.

7. *Postponements or Abandonment:*
The Race Committee in case of fog or heavy weather shall have the right to notify the contending yachts by 0900 (or 0800 should the warning signal be advanced to 1100 pursuant to Article 4) on the morning of a race not to leave their moorings until notified later, either (1) to proceed to the starting buoy or (2) that the race has been postponed for the day.

Except as above provided, the time of the warning signal shall not be postponed by the Race Committee except as follows:

a. In case of fog.
b. If, in its opinion, at the time appointed for the warning signal, the starting area is not sufficiently clear or the wind is too variable or too light or too strong or the sea too rough reasonably to test the relative speed of the two yachts.
c. In case a yacht, after she has left her mooring for the start of a race and before the warning signal, is in a serious collision or accident, not the result of a defect in her hull or in her sails, rigging, gear, or the handling thereof; or in case the Race Committee is notified before the warning signal that a person on board has been seriously injured after the yacht left her mooring for the start.

The Sailing Instructions shall specify the signals to be displayed in connection with postponements for the day or until later in the day. A copy of these Sailing Instructions shall be given to each yacht prior to the start of the Match.

The Race Committee may abandon a race as provided under Racing Rule 5.1(b) because of foul weather endangering the yachts or for other reasons directly affecting safety.

Under no circumstances may the course be shortened.

8. *Time Limit:*
If in any race neither yacht completes the first four legs in 3 hours 50 minutes, or if neither yacht completes the course in 5 hours 15 minutes, such race shall be resailed.

9. *Races Resulting in a Tie:*
A race resulting in a tie shall be resailed.

10. *Racing Rules of the International Yacht Racing Union to Govern:*
The Racing Rules of the International Yacht Racing Union as the same shall

exist at the time of the Races shall govern the Races, except insofar as the same may be inconsistent with other provisions of this Agreement, and particularly the provisions of Article 11 hereof, except that: Yachts are racing from the time of the warning signal.

Emergency running lights will be required equipment aboard each yacht.

11. *Communications:*
During a race, from the time of the warning signal for the start until the finish line has been crossed, a yacht shall not receive any prearranged communications or make use of any prearranged indications, such communications or indications not being available from the same medium to both yachts, as advice or assistance in handling the yacht during the race. While racing radio direction finders and Loran may be used but not Satellite or Omega or other similar navigational systems.

12. *Measurement Rule of the International Yacht Racing Union to Govern:*
The Measurement Rule of the International Twelve Metre Class as established by the International Yacht Racing Union effective March 1976 and amended November 1977, shall govern this Match. Only the Certificate of Classification issued by Lloyd's Register of Shipping shall be accepted in connection with Rule 26 of the Rating Rule.

Yachts shall comply in every respect with the requirements regarding construction and equipment contained in the Deed of Gift and the Interpretive Resolutions applying to national origin of design and construction.

Bilges shall be kept as reasonably dry as possible while racing.

No devices shall be fitted or employed which would permit the tilting of the mast athwartship.

13. No member of the Defender's crew may be a citizen of the country of the challenging club nor may a member of the crew of the challenging club be a citizen of the country of the defending club.

14. *Time Allowance:*
There shall be no time allowance.

15. *Rating:*
Yachts shall not rate over twelve metres.

16. *Selecting the Challenging Yacht:*
The challenging club shall have the right to name its yacht at any time,

provided that the notice of selection shall be received by the challenged club prior to 2400 (midnight) on September 11, 1980.

In the event that elimination races are held between yachts representing the Challenger and any one or more of the Royal Perth Yacht Club of Western Australia, the Royal Goteborg Yacht Club, the Royal Southern Yacht Club, the Royal Sydney Yacht Squadron and Société des Regates Rochelaises, and a yacht representing one of the five yacht clubs other than the Challenger is successful in the eliminations, the New York Yacht Club agrees to the substitution of that yacht club as the challenging yacht club and will accept its yacht if named as the Challenger prior to 2400 on September 11, 1980; and provided that such substituted yacht club shall agree to comply in all respects with the terms of these Conditions.

17. *Selecting the Defending Yacht:*
Prior to 2400 on September 11, 1980, the Challenger shall be informed of the yacht selected to defend the Cup.

18. *Accidents:*
(1) In case a serious accident occurs to either yacht prior to the warning signal, she shall have such time, not exceeding in any event four weeks, as the Committees representing the two Clubs shall determine to be reasonable to effect repairs before being required to start, or if such accident occur after the warning signal, before being required to start in the next race; but no such allowance of time to repair shall extend the Match beyond November 3, 1980.
(2) If either yacht, except as provided in Article 7, paragraph c, shall be disabled after leaving her mooring for the start of the race through a defect in her hull, or in her sails, rigging, gear or the handling thereof, the other yacht shall start and continue the race using her best endeavors to finish the race within the time limit; and if finished within the time limit, that race shall be won by that yacht.
(3) If through the fault of either yacht, the other be destroyed or so injured after the warning signal as to be incapable of repair in time to complete the Match before November 4, 1980, and the yacht so destroyed or injured is free from fault, the Match shall be awarded to her.

19. *Disqualification:*
If one yacht is disqualified in any race, such race shall be awarded to the other yacht, provided the race was completed within the time limit. The fouled yacht shall, however, be declared the winner if the Race Committee finds that her disablement caused by the foul prevented such completion.

20. *Representatives:*
Each Club shall by its Committee name a representative who shall have the right to be present at all measurements and shall have, when practicable, not less than twenty-four hours notice thereof. A representative of the Challenger shall have the right to be on board the Race Committee boat during the races and may be consulted by the Race Committee in regard to the matters referred to in Article 7. The respective representatives mentioned in this clause need not be the same person.

21. *Measurements:*
The Yacht Club d'Hyeres and the New York Yacht Club shall each select a measurer. These two, together with a Measurer appointed by the International Yacht Racing Union, shall constitute a Measurement Committee; and the decision of that Committee on questions of measurement and on questions of interpretation of the measurement rules shall be final. All potential challengers and defenders must be measured by this Committee prior to start of the respective August trials. All measurements, shall be taken or checked within two weeks of the commencement of the Match by the New York Yacht Club measurer, except that in lieu thereof the measurer may accept a certification in writing that no changes have been made affecting the certificate of rating previously issued by the Measurement Committee; and shall be filed with the Race Committee of the New York Yacht Club not less than three days before the first race. Displacement shall be checked by weighing and any measurement changes must be approved by the New York Yacht Club measurer.

22. *Re-Measurements and Inspections of Side Marks:*
If either yacht in any way changes her L. W. L. or sail plan as officially taken, she must obtain a re-measurement by special appointment before the next race and must report the alteration to the representative of the Measurement Committee and to the representatives of both clubs at the New York Yacht Club Station at Newport by 2100 of the day before the race following such alteration and must arrange with the Measurer for remeasurement and, if required, be in Brenton Cove by 0600, of the day of said race, and be at the disposition of the Measurer until 0700, if necessary for purposes of re-measurement.

If either yacht shall take in or remove ballast or dead weight, she must notify the Measurer and the representatives of the two clubs and be at the disposition of the Measurer for inspection of marks. The representatives of the two clubs shall have the right to be present at all re-measurements and inspections of marks and shall be given such notice thereof as time may permit; such notice shall be delivered to the Race Committee at Newport.

In the event that the Measurer is unable to obtain a measurement which is considered accurate before a race, a re-measurement shall be taken as soon as possible after the race; and a winning yacht so re-measured shall forfeit that race if she fails to rate Twelve Metres or less.

In the event that either yacht is out of the water and thereafter can not be launched in time to engage in the next scheduled race, because of weather conditions or for other causes beyond its control, the representatives of the New York Yacht Club and the challenging yacht club shall grant such yacht an additional day or days sufficient to allow such yacht to be launched and made ready for the next scheduled race.

Should either yacht desire to be hauled out, or should both yachts desire to be hauled out at the same time, either yacht or both yachts must have available to them a Measurer and adequate facilities; and, if such facilities or Measurer are not available to either yacht or to both yachts, sufficient time must be granted by the aforesaid representatives so that either yacht or both yachts will have available adequate facilities to haul out, be measured and be launched, and time within which to complete such a maneuver.

23. *Decisions of the Race Committee:*

The decisions of the Race Committee taken in consultation with the representative of the challenging club, as provided for in Article 20 and with respect to postponements and abandonment, shall be final and there shall be no appeal therefrom.

24. *International Jury:*

In addition there shall be an International Jury composed of not less than three individuals who are not nationals of the countries of either contesting club, which shall act on protests and interpretations of the racing rules deriving therefrom.

The decisions of the International Jury shall be final and there shall be no appeal therefrom.

YACHT CLUB D'HYERES
Marcel L. Bich, *Honorary Commodore*

NEW YORK YACHT CLUB
Henry H. Anderson, Jr., *Commodore*

October 2, 1979